MW01165660

Hop Gar Mantis Kung Fu

A Science of Combat

Steve Richards

Paul H. Crompton Ltd.

First edition 2000

Copyright (C) 1998 Steve Richards
ISBN : 1 874250 16 2
Published in the United Kingdom
by Paul H. Crompton Ltd.
94 Felsham Road,
London, sw15 1dq.
email: CROMPTONPH@aol.com

Gummerus Printing Jyväskylä, Finland 2000

To my wife Pauline Richards

and to my son

Gareth Patrick Richards -

the next generation!

Gareth Richards, 4 years, in 'Lama" Guard stance

Acknowledgements

Thanks are due to many people who have supported me over the years. I would like to to give special thanks to:

Mike & Mary Eveleigh,Tony Carpenter, Ian Palmer, Stuart Atkinson, Nick Liu,Terry McNee, Steve Hughes, Paul Traynor, Eddie Berry, Peter Collins, 'Ju-Jitsu John'; James Ho, Simon Wong, Brian McKinney, John Cain, Peter Nixon, Terry O'Neill, Dennis Martin, Paul Crompton, Peter Consterdine, Geoff Thompson and Roger D. Hagood

Also to my Chinese Masters:

Kenneth Liu - Franco Chun - Jimmy Chan - Lee-Sun-Wah - Samuel Kwok and Chung-Chi-Hung

And to my Closed Door Students and Approved Instructors:

Bill Wilson, Paul D'Ambrogio, Phil Mulvihill, Simon Dyu, Lung-Wan, Tim O'Sullivan

Main Photo Credits: Bill Wilson

Initial Graphic Design & Layout Assistant: Bill Wilson
Final Design & Layout: Liz Paton & Paul Crompton

Calligraphy - Nick Liu

Ars Requirit Totum Hominum

'The Art Requires The Whole Man'

DISCLAIMER

The author and publisher accept no liability whatsoever
for the unlawful or unethical use of the techniques,
methods or practices described or
illustrated in this book.

Readers are reminded of their responsibility always to
act within the law and to uphold the ethical spirit
of the martial arts.

Readers carry out the methods described and illustrated
in this book at their own risk. If you wish to study
and perform martial arts you should do so
with the help of a qualified instructor.

If you are in any doubt about your state of health you
should consult a physician or other health
advisor before training in the methods
presented in this book.

CONTENTS

FOREWORD - Peter Consterdine

There can only be a handful of people who are not born and bred Chinese who have as deep an understanding of Chinese Martial systems as does Steve Richards. So much so that he has been able to marry together two traditional systems and have the result approved by the senior Chinese Martial Arts community.

The uniqueness of his book, however, goes much deeper than simply whether or not two systems can work together. Rather it is an in-depth analysis of eastern Martial Arts from the standpoint of western science and western philosophy. By science, Steve includes not only physiology and biomechanics, but also psychology, and to a considerable extent. This approach holds a great appeal for me as it should for everyone, irrespective of their personal predisposition as to how martial arts is to be approached.

You would not expect to find Socrates as a focal point for better understanding the way to think and question our approach to the arts, but you will find it in this book.

At a glance you may think that 'post modernism to dialectical syncretism' is a subject which would send you running for cover, but don't let it. This book is unashamedly academic in its approach to how we should think about our martial arts, but despite how erudite it is, Steve never lets the reader down by not explaining clearly the meaning of such expressions.

This is therefore a challenging book, and, at times, I found myself disagreeing with certain premises that are strongly laid down. But that is part of the book's attraction - it makes us reconsider our own 'world view' and how we have shaped our individual 'empiricism', because we all have. If we feel strongly about a concept, and Steve does, it will likely have come through experiences which to us are 'empirical'.

This book takes an even bolder step, and that is into the world of practical Street Application of eastern martial arts. There are some excellent concepts and supporting psychology outlined and Steve's many years as a 'front line' Liverpool Police Officer gives his stance on his concepts all the credibility they need. He is not averse to the odd 'dig' at people who speak from other less 'official' front line occupations and there is a tendency to place doormen and pressure-point practitioners into convenient boxes which could be labelled 'emotional hypnotists'. This is another challenge of the book, because it is provocative yet at the same time it is very open and well written.

I found myself underlining sections of the manuscript with a marker pen and scribbling comments in the margins, which for me is a sign that I have been stimulated. I'm sure anyone who reads this work will be equally aroused. It is not a book purely about Chinese Martial Arts, but more about how we as individuals can think and argue more coherently about what we each experience through the practise and study of martial arts in general. I've always said that martial arts has become what I am, not what I do, and Steve's book goes a long way to explaining the 'how and why' of such a statement.

Author's Preface

As a child, my favourite heroes were from the Heroic and Classical eras of ancient Greece; stories of Alexander the Great and the famous Spartan 'Hoplite'* warriors. Best of all were the tales of Golden Mycenae, the fabulous city of King Agamemnon during the Trojan War period (circa 1200 BC). Archaeologists had discovered that the royal symbol of these ancient hero kings was a Golden Lion, a statue of which still stands at the Lion Gate entrance to the ruined city. This was the roaring lion of Greece!

Years later, when I first encountered Chinese martial arts, it was to be another Lion that caught my imagination; the one from the Tibetan Lion's Roar style of Kung-Fu. Although I have since studied other systems, this one will always be the closest to my heart. Born from Tibetan Buddhism, the system expresses an openness to freely absorbing techniques from other styles and cultures, whilst maintaining its essential core identity. Eventually, it produced offspring, including Tibetan Lama, Tibetan White-Crane and Hop-Gar (Hero's Family Fist).

Over the years I have been intrigued to learn how deep the hidden connections are that run between east and west. Indeed some historians have suggested that Alexander the Great introduced Greek martial arts into India, during the 4th century BC, and that these influenced the subsequent development of Indian, and then later Tibetan and Chinese, martial arts.

It is interesting to consider the symbol of the Lion in these matters. In ancient Greece, there were Lions (the same sub-species as found in India), but none at all in China, then or now. In Indian and Tibetan Buddhism, the Lion's Roar refers to the 'Breath of the Buddha'. In China there is of course the well known Lion Dance (performed only by martial arts students); and at the Emperor's Palace (the Forbidden City) in Beijing, images of Golden Lions stand guard.

Today, my own martial arts school is called Golden Lion Martial Arts Athletic Association, acknowledging my debt to Tibetan Lion's Roar, but also to the ancient Greeks. The Greeks were not only great soldiers, they were also philosophers and scientists. They recognised the importance of all high culture, and sought to understand the deep inter-connections between different civilisations. Thus, for me, the image of the Lion's Roar stands for a meeting of East and West at the deepest level of the human psyche. A roar started in Greece and returned enriched by the influences of Tibet and China.

(Hoplite is a term denoting a professional foot soldier)

Lion's Roar is a 'long-arm' system with predominantly circular movements and a full range of leg and ground fighting techniques...

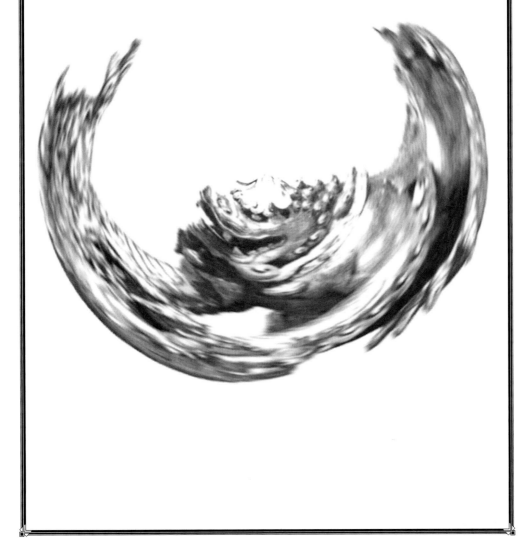

Introduction

This book is very different from most others dealing with the Chinese martial arts. In the past, most authors have tended to focus on either the artistic or the scientific aspects, without a marked attempt to synthesise the two into a higher level of understanding.

Although Kung-Fu originated in the East, it is now firmly embedded in the culture of the Western world, with its emphasis on science and practicality. The allure of the East has always included its supposed mystery and spirituality, which has compensated for the lack of such things found in the modern, technologically driven West. Today we find that the East has also 'moved' West, with the adoption of the scientific method and the western style market economy. So, it seems a blending of cultures was inevitable, with each taking from the other what it needed either to compensate for its own one sided-ness or to complement its already existing strengths.

These two factors, compensation and complementation describe the blending of two very different traditional martial arts systems into a new synthesis: Combined Hop-Gar Mantis Kung-Fu. Hop Gar, in its original form known as Lion's Roar, and the Lee-Yin-Sing branch of Bamboo Forest Temple Southern Praying Mantis, have never been written about in depth before, in the English language. Their synthesis is in keeping with Chinese tradition and has been augmented by the application of the best of western science and philosophical reasoning.

Both systems are built on principles, rather than mere technique or form, and although the techniques are very different in the two styles, even directly opposite to one another, their principles overlap in such a way that their union is ideal.

Lion's Roar is a 'long-arm' system, with predominantly circular movements, and a full range of leg and ground-fighting techniques. The Mantis is more linear and 'short-arm'. Both emphasise pressure and vital point attacks as fundamental. Lion's Roar energy is based on overwhelming momentum; the Mantis on explosive machine gun like shock power.

My Background

I was born in Liverpool in March 1957, and first took up the martial arts at the age of nine. I studied Shotokan and Wado-Ryu styles of Karate with my elder brother, and western boxing with my father, who had boxed for the Royal Navy in the 1930's. He had served as a boy-seaman in the far east,and there matured under pressure, fighting Chinese river pirates and bandits hand-to-hand. His love of China and the Chinese people endured until the end of his life.

At the age of fifteen, I seriously if rather precociously, undertook the private study of the various schools of depth psychology and psychotherapy (Sigmund Freud and Carl Gustav Jung). I had always been fascinated by the life of the psyche, recording my dream experiences from a very early age. This study was to run parallel with my martial arts, eventually cross-fertilising one another to produce a trans-cultural approach to the arts, informed by a knowledge of western depth psychology (the psychology of the unconscious) and classical philosophy. At sixteen I was introduced to authentic Chinese martial arts in Liverpool's Chinatown district. At that time (just prior to the Bruce Lee boom) it was very rare to find good teachers of traditional Kung-Fu arts. I had just met Kenneth Liu, who was to be my first true teacher, at a local technical college. I was extremely impressed by his fighting ability. For example, he had knocked out four attackers on a local railway station platform. They had been taunting him, by calling him 'Bruce Lee', and then picked a fight with him! This incident made him a minor celebrity at college, which he found rather uncomfortable. At that time, Si-Fu Liu was a very intense, rather 'brooding' young man, who didn't trust easily. Later he mellowed into one of the nicest and most friendly men I have ever known.

His fighting spirit was ferocious, honed in frequent real fights both in Hong Kong and in Liverpool. He was a good all round athlete (as were all his family) and insisted on supplementary fitness training, and what would today be called 'cross training' in other martial arts. As well as his core style, he also trained in Wing Chun under Joseph Cheng, frequently boxed,and practiced Judo with his elder brother Philip.

His younger brother Nick, also at the college, was a Wing Chun practitioner under Joseph Cheng and I first practiced Kung-Fu with him, finding the Wing Chun system both novel and interesting, compared to my own Karate and boxing background. However, it was Si-Fu Liu's own style that intrigued me the most. It was absolutely 'wild' and needed a high standard of fitness just to practice the basics. This system was the very rare Tibetan Lion's Roar which is the parent style of the Tibetan Lama, Hop Gar and White Crane styles. Si-Fu Liu's own teacher was Master Lau-Char-Chu, a South East Asia full contact champion, and martial arts instructor to the high security Stanley Prison staff in Hong-Kong.

Bruce Lee 'Connection'

I felt that I just had to learn this style. It had the dual attraction of being esoteric (Tibetan) and aggressively practical. Also, Si-Fu Liu's real life fighting experience and attitude gave it an unbeatable edge that other martial arts schools at that time just didn't seem to have. He and Nick tried to put me off. Westerners were just not accepted, and I should stay with Karate. This just made me more determined and persistent, and after a while they agreed to teach me. However, there were still 'tests'* like being led through all sorts of back streets and being told to wait until 'someone ' would meet me, and take me to the Kwoon (school). Although I didn't know it at the time, this school was the England Ching Wu Athletic Association, affiliated to the Hong -Kong Ching-Wu, and the famous Shanghai Ching-Wu, featured in the Bruce Lee film 'Fists of Fury'. It was also at that time one of the very few U.K. affiliated schools to the Hong Kong Chinese Martial arts Association.(1)

On arrival, I was put into a horse stance, whilst Si-Fu Liu lit a candle and told me to stay there until it melted. This kind of thing went on until they were satisfied that I was serious. They also insisted that as a former Karateka I should study Go-Ju Ryu style Karate at the same time, apparently because I could then appreciate the subtleties of Kung-Fu more fully! Dutifully, I did as I was told, although I couldn't really take to Go-Ju; for me the gap was becoming too large. At that time I was the only westerner (as a beginner) allowed to train, although some very senior international karateka based in the Merseyside area did train in

Wing Chun at the Ching-Wu, in an informal way. The other Si-Fu teaching at the school at this time were: Joseph Cheng (Wing Chun); Ho-Sing (Southern style Bamboo Forest Temple Mantis), and Philip Liu (Monkey Kung-Fu, Praying Mantis and Judo). Interestingly, in the light of current fashions, the Liu family always insisted on cross-training (2), believing that grappling, boxing and all round athleticism were essential ingredients for the well-rounded fighter. All three brothers worked in Philips' Chinese restaurant, and got plenty of practical practice as they called it, after 'kicking-out' time, at the local pubs and clubs. I used to go over to watch the fights, whilst enjoying a 'T' bone steak!

The training was very hard. You were expected to learn the correct tradition and to fight full contact, every session. This involved gloving and padding up, sometimes in Chinese leather and bamboo body armour (always a bad sign!) and fighting all-out with anything and everything. Weight categories were non-existent, and no concessions were given for differences in skill levels. On one occasion, I was gloved up in an open field to face an animal of a Liverpool taxi driver called 'Norman' who was five stones heavier than me, and a very experienced street fighter. There are no 'rope escapes' in a field and other than running away, I had to go for it. You learn a lot about yourself and your art from such encounters. Later during one such free fight, Si-Fu Liu grappled me into an arm lock and broke my elbow joint. I was still expected to carry on however, and it took several years for me to get back a full range of movement into the joint. This was despite western and Chinese orthopaedic medicine, and herbal treatments.

Often, there were 'invited guests' from other styles, sometimes even other countries. Once I found myself in an apparent 'grudge match' with an American kick-boxer, who believed 'limeys' (his expression) were fair game. He was a good kicker, he just couldn't punch, and he didn't like 'limeys' - English people - or having his long blond hair used as a lever for take-downs or being 'shin dropped' in the groin. Nevertheless, we parted company as 'friends'. In 1974, at the age of seventeen, I joined Merseyside Police as a Cadet. I did this because decision time had come about a career. Up until then, I was going to follow my father into the Royal Navy, but that would have meant the end of my martial arts studies. So, I joined the Police. Its self defence training was markedly unim-

Steve Richards with his first teacher, Si-Fu Kenneth Liu

pressive. Later, on joining the regular force, I found myself up against the force boxing instructor at the Ryton Police training College, near Coventry. He asked me to 'spar' with head gear and so forth so that he could try out my Kung-Fu against his Western boxing. I was much lighter than he, and he had his status to maintain, before an 'audience' of curious Policemen. What he didn't know was that I trained for full contact sparring all the time, back in Liverpool, and wasn't at all intimidated. I remembered Si-Fu Liu's teachings, 'switched' into attack mode, and flattened him. To his credit, the boxing instructor took it well, and there were no recriminations, despite his loss of face.

In 1975, as a 'rookie cop', I took up the Hung-Gar style of Kung-Fu, under Master Jimmy Chan, again at the Ching-Wu in Liverpool. I took with me the mantle of 'Dai-Si-Hing' (eldest Kung-Fu brother), which Master Chan acknowledged until his death in 1989. This conferred the immediate status of being his most senior non-Chinese student. I enjoyed the powerful Hung-Gar system, with its emphasis on proper positioning, and precise footwork. Hung-Gar is perhaps the exemplar system of good traditional Chinese Kung-Fu. It is the foremost of the five family styles of southern Shaolin boxing, and develops good ethics and morality as well as martial technique. I realised early on that the secret to its successful practical application lay in the ability to mechanically practice 'proper form' and then to utilise this as a chassis for the delivery of clean and efficient techniques.

Ching-Wu Influences

Good technical practitioners of this style are actually very rare. The classical forms are difficult and lengthy, which encourages some

The 'Rookie' cop -
(author standing third from right).

students to rush through them, becoming unbalanced and developing the bad habit of not finishing techniques properly. It's easy to imagine what this would mean in a 'live situation'! In the early to mid seventies, I wrote and had published in 'Karate & Oriental Arts' (KOA) magazine published and edited by Paul Crompton, some of the earliest and at the time most authoritative English language articles on Chinese Kung-Fu. These covered the Tibetan Lion's Roar, Hung-gar and the Ching-Wu Association itself. The articles generated a lot of interest, but at the time, membership of the Liverpool Ching-Wu for westerners was strictly by invitation only. This meant that the Chinatown location of the school was not openly advertised, and prospective students had to make a special effort to find it. Even then, people were vetted carefully, and had to serve a probationary period. This helped to create an open and friendly atmosphere, accepting of people, regardless of background, who had proved themselves to be of good or 'reformed character'. The Chinese Si-Fu actually taught in the belief that their teaching could make a difference and help to turn someone's life around, and away perhaps from either crime or despair. In some cases these beliefs were justified. Fund-raising for charity was a major goal in these times, and the school itself was managed by the members (of all grades and status) fairly and democratically.

During the 1975-1977 period, the Ching-wu flourished, with many different styles and teachers freely coming and going. Each night of the week, it was an 'open house' with Si-fu's turning up and teaching their respective styles openly and without bias. The Ching-Wu ethos was that no prejudice was to be shown against any martial art, whatever its ethnic root. Perhaps uniquely for a Chinese school, the Ching-Wu associations around the world actively encourage the simultaneous practice of Japanese styles, alongside Chinese ones, under the same roof, and with the same students. Of course individual bias can never be surgically removed, but the positive attitude was honestly held and expressed, to the undoubted benefit of all. Some of today's 'cross trainers' might find something of value in this, as the darker side of 'eclecticism'; the mere 'stealing of techniques', abstracted from their cultural context, did not happen.

In 1977, Kenneth Liu left to pursue a career in pharmacology, and mas-

Master Chan with Steve Richards - his senior student 1975 - 1980

ter Chan opened his own school, the Liverpool Hung Gar Kung Fu Friendship Association. The Ching-Wu closed, and almost by default I continued my studies of Hung Gar and Northern Shaolin under Master Chan.

My interest in depth psychology had continued through these years. I also seriously studied Buddhism, joining the Buddhist Society in London, and becoming a committed vegetarian. In the Police I was getting a lot of practical fighting experience, some of it against fellow Police Officers! At that time, I was the only 'Kung-Fu Cop' in the Merseyside force, and martial artists even from other systems were a rarity. It just wasn't the done thing to be a Buddhist, non-drinking, non-smoking vegetarian and be into that 'David Carradine Stuff'. Still, I persisted with my beliefs and principles, occasionally re-educating a colleague about his manners along the way!

During my Police career, I was assaulted many times in the line of duty. I was attacked with knives and petrol bombs, I faced armed assailants, was 'jumped' by gangs, attacked by doormen, had dogs set on me, went through riots, got hospitalised with head injuries and had many other encounters in the violent side of my job. As experience it was certainly invaluable and it led to a refinement of realistic skills, that could perhaps not have been gained in any other arena.

As time went by, more and more martial artists joined the force, and it became an enjoyable thing to work with them in the 'front line'. Some I knew I could trust with my life, as indeed happened on more than one occasion. The shared martial arts background bonded us together even more strongly than being colleagues in the Police. Having someone with you who would back you 'unto death' in a crisis is a great feeling. So thanks to John R.; I will never forget.

In 1982, I decided to formalise my psychology training, and started an Open University degree course. I had started working as an 'assistant' with a Western 'Spiritual Healer', in 1980, and also did voluntary psychiatric social work at a local hospital, to give some practical background to my degree. Also in 1980, I had left Master Chan to study Southern style Bamboo Forest Temple Mantis Kung-Fu. This was the very rare Lee-Yin-Sing branch of the system. In all, I was to have five teachers of this style over the next ten years, including training with Grandmaster Lee-Sun-wah, son of the founder: Great-Grand-Master Lee-Yin-Sing. In 1987, I finally left the Police in order to pursue a fuller career in the martial arts and in the health care professions. In 1988, together with my good friend Brian

Grandmaster Lee-Sun-Wah (seated right)
Si-Fu Lee-Po (seated left)
Si-fu James Ho (standing right)
Si-Fu Steve Richards (standing left)

McKinney, and the late Chinese Master Jifu Huang, I helped to establish the British Chin Woo (Ching-Wu) Athletic Association. Also at this time, I met the Wing-Chun and Tibetan White Crane Kung-Fu teacher Samuel Kwok, and we became close friends, frequently training together. I respect Sam greatly, and regard him as among the best of his generation.

In 1989, during Master Jimmy Chan's final illness, Master Kwok and I visited him in hospital, where he told Samuel Kwok that I was the 'eldest Si-Hing' under him, and asked that Sam 'look after' my further Kung-Fu development, handing me over to him as his student. This was a great honour for me, and a very touching moment. Master Chan was a truly good person,

Grandmaster Lee-Sun-Wah, with Si-fu Richards, 1988

who worked tirelessly to raise money for charities through his martial art career. He was very well loved in the Chinese community. Master Chan respected Sam's ability and character most highly, and true to his word Sam still keeps a watchful eye over my training, and my development as a person.

Today, I am proud to be a recognised teacher of Wing-Chun Kung-Fu under his instruction and guidance, and also to be able to further my understanding of the Tibetan martial arts. It is my firm belief that the teacher is ultimately more important than the style, and this is my motivation for studying with him.

Around 1988, I first began to put together a 'combined' syllabus for the Hop-Gar (Lion's Roar) and Praying Mantis styles. These two systems suited my personality and practical experience, and seemed almost made to complement each other. The syllabus was recognised by the Amateur Martial Association (AMA) and formed the basis for the later development of an official Combined Hop-Gar Mantis style.

In 1991, I retired from the public teaching of martial arts, continuing to act as mentor and guide for the development of my closed door students. In 1988, I had started to study Occupational Therapy, but had left to pursue formalised training in psychotherapy and hypnosis. Professionally, I became involved at the very heart of the psychotherapy, hypnotherapy, counselling and complementary medicine fields. I published research and professional papers at international conferences,and in professional journals. I established a new school of psychotherapy: Psycho-Systems Analysis and a new methodological approach to philosophy known as Dialectical Syncretism. I became a consultant psychotherapist and respiratory psychophysiologist to the National Health Service and in private practice. I also became a consultant to the British Council for Complementary Medicine, writing the admission criteria for their register of professional practitioners.

Then in 1996, I felt ready to teach publicly once again; I renewed affiliation to the AMA and after assessment was awarded the grade of 6th Dan in the combined Hop-Gar Mantis style. I also approached the British Council for Chinese Martial Arts (BCCMA) the Sports Council governing body, and they assessed both me and the Combined Hop-Gar Mantis system as authentic.

My work as a psychotherapist and psychophysiologist, and my career as a martial artist, has been recorded in Who's Who in America (World, Science, and Medicine editions). I believe that I am the first martial artist to have been so honoured.

In 1999, I at last renewed my association with the Hung-Gar style, by

Master Samuel Kwok (r) ready to conduct the 'indoor ceremony' into the Wing Chun Kung fu family for Si-Fu Richards, 1988

becoming the student of Master Chung-Chi-Hung of the Wong-Fei-Hung Institute, China. I had known Master Chung for some eleven years already, and was very impressed by the range and depth of his knowledge, as well as his unconditional support and friendship for me right from the beginning of our association. His knowledge in Hung-Gar Kung-Fu is unrivaled, which was acknowledged in China by his becoming the technical director of the Institute named after Hung-Gar's most famous practitioner Master Wong-Fei-Hung. His role includes the recovery of the complete system and its re-establishment in the Peoples' Republic of China. I can think of no better qualified instructor, both technically and

personally, for this system, and think it a great honour to be accepted as his student. Further, I am continuing my study of the Lam-Sang branch of Jook-Lum Temple Mantis, under Si-fu Roger D. Hagood (U.S.A.), an indoor disciple of Senior Masters Harry Sun Si-Bak, Wong-Bak-Lim and Gin-Foon-Mark.

In 1998, I re-established links with my old friend Brian McKinney, whom I respect as undoubtedly one of the very finest western exponents of the Chinese martial arts. Together with Si-Fu Kenneth Liu, Brian and I are working towards the further growth and development of the British Chin Woo Athletic

Roger D. Hagood

Master Chung-Chi-Hung of the Wong-Fei-Hung Institute, China, teacher of Hung Gar Kung Fu to his new pupil Steve Richards, 1988

Association. I now teach a number of syllabuses derived from the full breadth of my experience in Chinese Martial arts: Hung-Gar Kung-Fu: under Master Chung-Chi-Hung, Technical Director of the Wong-Fei-Hung Institute, China; Wing-Chun Kung-Fu: under Master Samuel Kwok, Yip-man lineage; Jook-Lum Temple Praying Mantis Kung-Fu, under Grand-Master Lee-Sun-Wah, Lee-Yin-Sing branch. Founder of

Combined Hop-Gar Mantis Kung-Fu: BCCMA U.K. Sports Council Governing Body for Chinese Martial arts, and the Amateur Martial Arts Association (A.M.A.)

In July 1998, at Manchester Metropolitan University I presented two scientific papers to an international conference on martial arts research entitled "Hyperventilation: Trance states and Suggestion in the martial arts"; and, "From Post-modernism to Dialectical Syncretism: understanding the anthropology and cultural evolution of martial arts systems". Both papers were subsequently published and copies housed at the university.

The Combined Hop-gar Mantis system arises directly from the sum of all of my experiences in Kung-Fu, and the broader context of martial arts over a period of thirty-three years. It is I hope a tribute to the superlative quality of my teachers, particularly Grand-Master Lee-Sun-Wah, Master Samuel Kwok and Si-Fu Kenneth Liu.

My thirteen years practical experience, and empirical 'pressure testing' in the real arena of Police work in Liverpool, allowed me to understand the deeper principles of Chinese Kung-Fu, and more importantly, how they should be taught, realistically, to others. Being a westerner, educated in science and philosophy, I was in a unique position to assimilate the best of East and West, without compromise with either. Not subjecting myself to false modesty, I can say the result is an very effective synthesis of traditional Chinese Kung-Fu and western science.
:
The aim of this book is not merely to portray a 'tradition', there are plenty of other works that achieve only that. Rather its purpose is to communicate the principles of combat and philosophy that underlie this most efficient system of Combined Hop Gar Kung Fu.

The 'secret' of applying traditional Kung-Fu in the street is *an understanding of your system's guiding principles*. This understanding must be thorough, and never taken for granted. It must be earned through hard work, intelligence, and continuous pressure testing. The principles and experiences presented in this book will prepare you for real combat, and for personal growth, through the practice of your martial art, regard-

*Over several generations
the Tibetan Lion's Roar
developed into the
now distinct
systems of
White Crane,
Hop Gar
and
Lama...*

less of style or system.

For those who may be interested in the more classical elements of Hop-Gar Mantis, or who wish to see the techniques, a series of quality digital video tapes is being produced.

Now, read on, open your heart... and your mind!

 (1) The testing of an applicant for training in a Kung fu school is a tradition, using different methods, depending on the teacher.

(2) In general, a teacher did not want his students to study other styles whilst training at his style. Since the time of Bruce Lee, more and more students have taken to cross-training, i.e. taking from several styles.

History

Chinese martial arts systems have origin myths, generally accepted stories, transmitted by word and in writing, that account for the origin and development of the 'style'. For the most part, these are a mixture of historical fact and elaboration, often used to legitimise a particular master's lineage, and therefore his or her teachings.

The emerging discipline of **martial arts anthropology** (the scientific study of the cultural origins and practice of the martial arts) has revealed the basic structural similarity in these stories, and how they are related in form to other kinds of collective, cultural narratives, such as the hero myth, which is found universally around the world, and throughout history.

Many 'traditional' Chinese systems have origin myths that suggest a kind of mystical revelation or intuition, on the part of the style's founder, connected with the observation of an animal or animals, and how this experience led to the development of a new human fighting art. Martial arts anthropologists must, of course, take note of these culturally transmitted and legitimised narratives when tracing the 'true' development of the system. However, there is another analytical method available which can reveal just as much about the evolution of a given martial arts style. **This is the analysis of form.**

Form As A Clue To Origin

'Form' here means not kata or pattern of sequential movements, but the actual movements, postures and techniques that make up the system itself. From these, it is possible to make comparisons with other examples of martial arts styles, and deduce lineage and cross-fertilisation that may have occurred in the past. As a modern example, just consider the known relationship between Japanese Karate and Korean Tae-Kwon-Do. Purely through an analysis of form, it is possible to establish that a connection between the two has occurred, even without a knowledge of their respective histories, or origin myths.

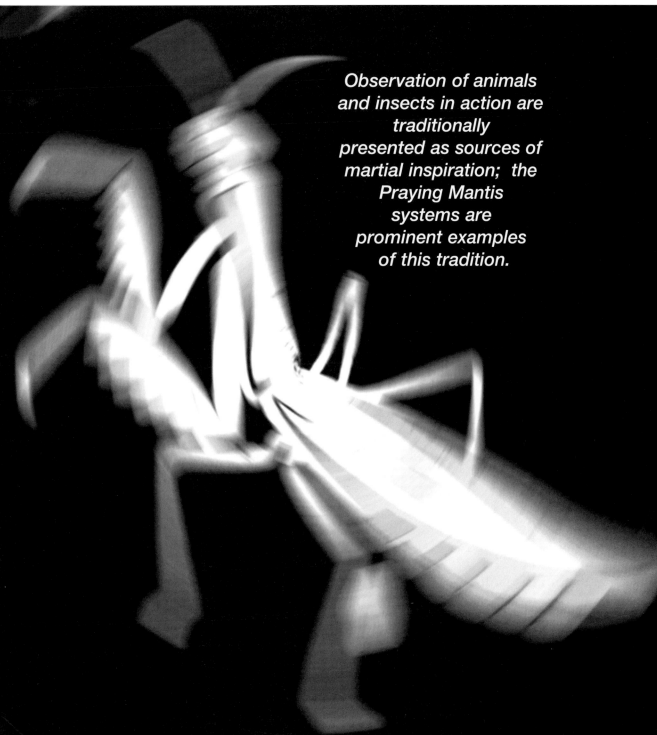

Observation of animals and insects in action are traditionally presented as sources of martial inspiration; the Praying Mantis systems are prominent examples of this tradition.

Some Chinese systems are open about a different cultural dynamic at work in their development. For example, the Southern Choy Lay Fut style is a self acknowledged synthesis of systems that have gone before. Albeit the newly synthesised style is somewhat different from any one of its 'parent' systems. **Therefore, the new style appears to be more than just the sum of its component parts,** and to have evolved into something quite separate. Nevertheless, a structural analysis of form reveals the originating connection sufficiently clearly to satisfy the rigour of an anthropological analysis.

Nowadays a third developmental trend in traditional Chinese martial arts has arisen. This is the so-called combined style. **Combined styles start from the premise that two or more systems may be joined together in such a way as to complement one another.** Often, the systems (there are usually two) also compensate for each other's weaknesses, although this aspect is seldom emphasised, so as not to cause offence to the elder generations of masters. **Typically, you will find the systems combined according to the polarity principle of 'opposites', so loved in Chinese thought.** For example, the soft or internal Yang style of Tai-Chi has been combined by my friend Si-Fu Simon Wong with the hard, more external Chow's family Praying Mantis, to make 'Yellow Dragon Combined Tai-Chi Mantis'. The Southern Mantis style has also been recently, and successfully, combined with Hung-Gar, to create 'Steel-Wire Mantis'. Likewise, this book is concerned with such a new combined style, created from two very rare systems: Tibetan Lion's Roar (Hop-Gar), and the Lee-Yin-Sing lineage of Southern Bamboo Forest Temple Praying Mantis.

Combined Styles

Let's now look at the mythic and historical origins of the two parent systems, and then more closely at the origin of the combined Hop-Gar Mantis style itself.

It is usual, when considering the history and development of Chinese styles, to divide them up between large opposed groupings of systems; for example, internal and external, northern and southern, Buddhist and Taoist and so on. However, there are other classifications in use, for example the 'family' styles, and those centred around 'tribe' or 'ethnic group. **One group however is in general missing from standard classification, and this is the Tibetan.**

Tibet occupies a unique geographical position, straddling the Himalayas and lying at the juncture of two vast and ancient cultures: those of India and China.   Culturally, Tibet's relatively recent history has been dominated by Buddhism, and by its relationship politically to China. Although Tibetan 'Lama' Buddhism is well known, the fact that there is a strong tradition of Lama martial arts is less well known.   Those that are known arose in similar mythic circumstances to the Buddhist (Shaolin) styles of China; that is, **through the observation of animals by monks in a meditative state.**

Lion's Roar

During the Ming dynasty, the dominant Han peoples of China oppressed the minority ethnic groupings of Tibet, Manchuria and Mongolia.   The latter groups were treated as third class citizens, and used as a cheap source of labour. However, in 1644 AD, the Ming dynasty was overthrown by the Manchurian Ching.   For the next 276 years, China was in a constant state of rebellion, as the deposed Mings sought to regain power.

The Shaolin sect of Buddhism had deep connections with the Han, so allied themselves with the Ming rebels. As is well known, the Shaolin temples became training centres for revolutionaries, the famous Shaolin open hand and fist salute still seen today standing for 'the Ming shall overcome the Ching!' The Ching ruling classes sought masters of martial arts capable of defeating the warrior Shaolin monks. They turned to the Tibetan monasteries for help, and found that the Lamas would offer instruction to the Emperor's imperial bodyguard, but that they would not become involved in fighting fellow Buddhist monks, directly.   Thus, the martial arts of Tibet were to become the Imperial Kung-Fu of China!

The origin of the Tibetan Lion's Roar (Hop-Gar) system, is said to have been back in the Ming dynasty, with an ethnic Chinese called Ah-Dat-Tor-Lama.   Very little is known for sure about Ah-Dat-Tor, different versions of the tradition add or delete details, but there is some evidence that he originally hailed from Kwangsi province, in south-western China. The origin myth states that one day, as Ah-Dat-Tor Lama was meditating on a hillside, he had a 'vision' of an ape and a crane locked in desperate combat. The ape attacked quickly and deceptively, with powerful circular blows, tumbling and grabbing (grappling) techniques. The crane responded with equal speed, employing its feet, wings and beak, in graceful, skilled and deadly accurate attacks.

Eventually, the crane struck the ape in the eye. The ape fled and the crane flew away, leaving Ah-Dat-Tor Lama inspired to create a new martial art style, based on a combination of the techniques of the two animals. He became determined to develop his new system as an overwhelming martial art, full of grace, aggression and deception. **He named it the Lion's Roar, (Si-Ji-Hao) after the 'Breath of the Buddha'.**

The name 'Lion's Roar' held for the next several generations of Tibetan Lama martial arts masters. However, Ah-Dat-Tor's original style was undergoing continuous revision, as it encompassed more and varied techniques. Originally, Ah-Dat-Tor had compiled a series of classifications based on the number 'eight'. There were to be eight fundamental stances, footwork patterns, kicks, punches, all built around core principles. The principles were to determine techniques, which in effect were just delivery systems for **'overwhelming power'.**

As time went on, the Lion's Roar martial art was introduced into Ah-Dat-Tor's home province of Kwangsi. Here it took on the 'new' name of Lama Kung-Fu, after the monks who introduced it. However, by this time the original system had developed so much, that there were already clearly distinct versions in use. One was to become known as Tibetan White Crane. This system placed emphasis on the crane techniques rather than the ape techniques. The version of the system still calling itself Lion's Roar had much more ape than crane, so already a dissolution was setting in.

Years later, a master of the Lion's Roar martial art, called Wong Yin Lum, a student of the Tibetan Monk Sing-Lung, set up a 'fighting stage' in

Canton province, southern China. There he challenged any and all of Canton's masters to defeat him. Many tried, but all were beaten (this is a matter of accepted history even in other styles, so therefore accurate). Wong-Yin-Lum was elected to the number one position of the Canton 'Ten Tigers' (top Kung-Fu masters) as a result of his famous victories on the fighting stage.

Wong Yin Lum later re-named his version of Lion's Roar as Hop-Gar, meaning 'Hero or Patriot's' Family style'. Over the next several generations, the Tibetan Lion's Roar evolved still further into the now distinct styles of Lama, White Crane and Hop Gar, with some people still referring to their style by the original name

Today, masters and grand-masters for these systems may be found in China, Hong-Kong and the United States. In New York, some Lama stylists, Si-Fus David Ross, and Steve Ventura, have attempted to draw together all of the strands of the separate traditions to re-constitute both the original system, and to develop a 'modern' Lama Kung-Fu. In Great Britain, the original Lion's Roar has been 'combined' by this author, with the rare and secret Bamboo Forest Temple Praying Mantis.

Bamboo Forest Temple Mantis

Southern Praying Mantis Kung-Fu is a generic (collective) name for a whole grouping of related styles that themselves are a part of a larger ethnically based family of systems. **The usual mistake westerners make is to think of the southern Mantis as being related to the family of northern Chinese Praying Mantis styles.** Actually, they are not only very different, but also entirely unrelated, with separate origins. The 'northern' Mantis styles are very much in the character of northern Shaolin Kung-Fu, and historically have shown an openness to absorbing techniques from other systems.

Southern Mantis Kung-Fu has arisen ethnically from the 'Hakka' people, found predominantly today in the south-western Chinese province of Kwangsi (Cantonese). Some variants of the southern Mantis claim descent from Shaolin, but others claim a Taoist origin. The most well known and propagated version of southern Mantis is the Chow's family or Chow-Gar Tong-Long (Mantis). Others include 'Chu-Gar' (Chu Family) and the 'Iron Ox' Mantis systems. Related 'Hakka' Kung-Fu systems include Pak-Mei (White Eyebrow) and Lung-Ying-Kuen (Dragon Boxing). Until fairly recent times, these Hakka systems were not taught even to Chinese, unless they were of Hakka descent. Nowadays, the old taboos and restrictions are giving way, although one southern Mantis style, 'Bamboo Forest Temple', is still rare even in Chinese circles, let alone amongst Westerners.

There is (of course!) disagreement over which is the original Mantis system, but the origin myth passed down through the Bamboo Forest lineage makes a very strong claim to originality and pre-eminence. From my own personal research into the style's history, there seem to be at least two versions of the Bamboo Forest Temple Mantis. The most well known can be considered as the 'original', and hailed directly from the Bamboo Forest Temple in Kwangsi province, during the 18th century. This version is represented in the United States by Harry Sun Si-Bak, and masters Wong-Bak-Lim and Gin-Foon Mark (one of Bruce Lee's many teachers), and in England by Grandmaster Kim-Law, grandstudent of Wong-Yuk-Gong.

Grandmaster Lee-Yin-Sing

The other branch was developed during the middle of the 20th century by Great Grandmaster Lee-Yin-Sing. Lee-Yin-Sing was an accomplished Kung-Fu master of the Hung-Gar and Chu -Gar Mantis styles, living and practicing in the Hong-Kong New Territories. The origin myth, as passed down by his family, goes as follows.

One day a monk known as Lee-Tik visited Master Lee-Yin-Sing's school. Master Lee took pity on the monk, who seemed poor and without food, and offered him shelter and meals. The monk liked to watch the Kung-fu classes, but gave nothing away about his own background. Master Lee was suspicious, and thought that the monk may know something, but Lee-Tik remained silent on this matter, and just watched.(1)

Eventually, the time came for Lee-Tik to leave. He thanked Master Lee, and as he was parting happened to say that Master Lee's Kung-Fu was not much good!   Master Lee was a proud man, already with a reputation as a fighter. He challenged the monk who obliged by defeating him effortlessly.   Lee-Tik told Master Lee that he was from the Jook-Lum (Bamboo Forest) temple, in Kwangsi, and that he had used the temple's Mantis style to defeat him. Master Lee recognised the highest level of Kung-Fu skill in the monk, and begged him to teach him.   Lee-Tik said that he was returning to Kwangsi, and that the only way for him to learn was to come with him right away. Lee-Yin-Sing left with the monk, without telling anyone, even his family, and effectively 'disappeared' for the next six years.

When he returned, he announced that he had 'mastered' the Jook-Lum Mantis, and promptly embarked on a challenge match enterprise against all-comers to prove his skills.   He gained a reputation as a fierce Mantis boxer, and was a contemporary of Wing-Chun's Grandmaster Yip-Man. He was a colourful character, who became well known if not notorious amongst Hong-Kong's Kung-Fu elite.   Grandmaster Gin-Foon-Mark told me personally that although he considered his own branch of Jook-Lum Mantis as the original, he had known Great Grandmaster Lee-Yin-Sing and accepted that he had indeed returned to the Kwangsi province temple, and there learned a 'different' version of the system.   Grandmaster Mark also added that he believed that Lee-Yin-Sing went on to become a movie-star in Singapore, before disappearing once again, this time into Vietnam!

The Lee-Yin-Sing version of Jook-Lum Temple Mantis is very 'cut-down' and based on principles, and fighting practice rather than forms.   His own students were a very hard lot, frequently fighting in Taiwan in no-holds barred contests. The current Grandmaster of this branch of the style is Lee-Sun-Wah of Liverpool (U.K.) he is Lee-Yin-Sings son. I have been fortunate to have had five teachers of this style, and most privileged to be able to claim Grandmaster Lee amongst them.

Origin of the Combined Style

The origin of the combined Hop-Gar Mantis system, goes back to 1973, with the arrival in Liverpool England, from Hong-Kong, of Si-Fu Kenneth Liu. Si-Fu Liu was a student of Tibetan Lion's Roar Kung-

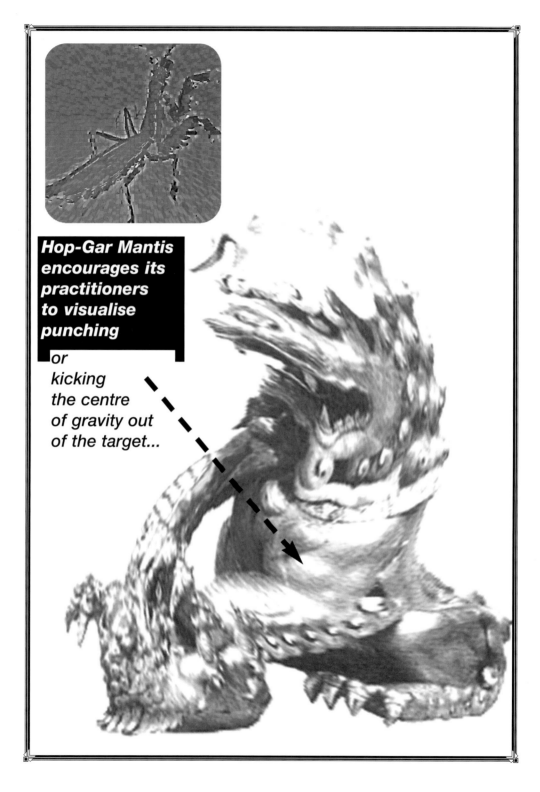

Hop-Gar Mantis encourages its practitioners to visualise punching

or
kicking
the centre
of gravity out
of the target...

Fu, and a teacher of southern style Lion Dancing. I began training under Si-Fu Liu at Liverpool's Ching-Wu Athletic Association, a branch of the Hong Kong Ching Wu and Hong Kong Chinese Martial Arts Associations. I studied under Si-Fu Liu for four years, until professional commitments (Si-Fu Liu was a western trained pharmacist, as well as qualifying in mainland China in acupuncture and traditional Chinese medicine) meant that he had to stop teaching. I continued on with my studies of Kung-Fu under Master Jimmy Chan (Hung-Gar and Northern Shaolin) for six years, becoming his most senior non-Chinese student (Dai-Si-Hing). Still, I could never forget my love for my first Chinese style: Lion's Roar, and during my time with Master Chan, I was known as 'The Hop-Gar man', despite my seniority in the Hung-Gar school.

I published the first articles in English, on the Lion's Roar Kung-Fu, in Karate & Oriental Arts magazine (KOA) in 1976, (April , September & December editions). I went on to write on Hung-Gar (1977 & 1979) in KOA and 'Fighters' magazines. Later in the 1980's I was to appear again in Fighters and 'Combat' magazines, this time writing the first English language articles on the Lee-Yin-Sing Mantis system.

In 1980, I had been formally introduced to the Jook-Lum Mantis style, by my Lion's Roar, and Hung-Gar Si-Dai (younger brother): Eddie Berry. I had already encountered this system before, in 1973, but I had not then been experienced enough to recognise its potential, and had effectively overlooked it. This time however, its real effectiveness began to dawn on me. Eddie Berry became my 'guide' and 'first door' to the style, through which I was to receive instruction over the next ten years from four Chinese teachers, culminating in Grandmaster Lee-Sun-Wah, son of the founder, Lee-Yin-Sing.

My thirteen years practical experience as a Liverpool police officer, allowed me to develop a keen awareness of what was functional, in the face of all manner of violent assaults, with empty hands and weapons, from single to multiple attackers. I was able to learn 'the hard way' through defeats as well as victories, the relative importance and functionality of such things as 'trapping' and ground fighting; and at last, after years of such experience, I felt able to formulate my own combined system, based on the sum of all of my master's teachings.

I chose the name 'Hop-Gar Mantis' for the new style. Hop-Gar was selected instead of the original name of Lion's Roar, because the Hop-Gar name was well known amongst Kung-Fu circles, and was connected with me personally, by name, in the Liverpool Chinese community.

Both 'parent systems' to the combined style had started out in the 'tradition' of absolute practicality. The new synthesis honours this tradition in the context of our contemporary times.

The style has been authenticated as genuine Chinese Kung-Fu by the U.K. Sports Council governing body, the British Council for Chinese Martial Arts (BCCMA) and by the Amateur Martial Associations (AMA). Hence the system is internationally recognised, including in mainland China itself.

(1) It is common, even traditional one might say, for a Kung fu Master to keep his cards close to his chest about what he knows .

HOP GAR MANTIS: COMBAT PRINCIPLES

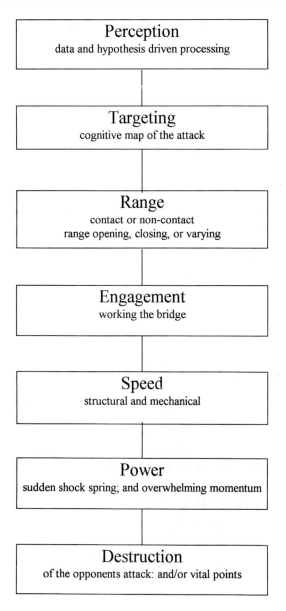

Perception
data and hypothesis driven processing

Targeting
cognitive map of the attack

Range
contact or non-contact
range opening, closing, or varying

Engagement
working the bridge

Speed
structural and mechanical

Power
sudden shock spring; and overwhelming momentum

Destruction
of the opponents attack: and/or vital points

The guiding principles of the combined Hop-Gar Mantis system

© **S.T.Richards 1999**

Principles

The combined Hop-Gar Mantis style is built around a nucleus of core principles that determine the application and function of the entire system. Many martial arts claim that they are based on guiding principles, but few if any manage to synthesise Eastern art with Western science and philosophy.

I quite deliberately place the term 'philosophy' in with Western science, which may surprise some readers, who have perhaps, come to think of the oriental martial arts as philosophical. **In fact, the term philosophy is Greek, and means 'love of wisdom'.** What is known as 'eastern philosophy' is in the main (with exceptions of course!) concerned with religious rather than the logical or rational subjects, so I wish to make it quite clear that when I speak of philosophy I am referring to western style reasoning, and logic. **Sadly, it is all too common amongst many western practitioners of the oriental martial arts to misunderstand and reject their own philosophical heritage, and so lose three thousand years of culture through sheer lack of thought.**

Therefore, the principles of the Hop-Gar Mantis system are here presented in such a way as to unite rather than to divide the complementary cultures of East and West. This is the best way for martial arts knowledge to take root; that is, in familiar soil. **Otherwise, we become mere sad 'imitators' of an alien culture, doomed to be superficial.**

There was a time, between the third and first centuries BC, when East and West did meet, and exchanged cultures productively for all. This was the 'Hellenistic Age', the period following Alexander the Great's' establishment of a Greek empire, that stretched from the Adriatic sea to the Indian ocean. From this period, in modern Afghanistan, statues of Buddha have been discovered wearing Greek toga's, and with facial features which are clearly Greek!

A new philosophical movement arose, that of syncretism which effec-

Mantis boxers focus on the shoulder area as the main initiating source of attack at close range. Eye to eye gaze is distracting and slows reactions down.

tively meant the blending of opposites, based on the principle of a deep similarity or complementarity, between ideas, or things, but usually disguised by superficial differences. Hellenistic syncretism worked to discover higher level truths, and towards the establishment of a cosmopolitan world.

Dialectic

Another significant contribution from Greek thought is a method of dealing with 'opposites' known as the dialectic. Early Greek philosophers of the Ionian school (circa 600 BC) understood the concept of 'duality' in nature, and the dynamic interplay of opposite energies or forces. This is of course familiar to martial artists through the concepts of yin and yang. **The dialectic, is essentially a way of discovering truth through 'reasoning'.** This reasoning may be mental, and/or physical.

Similar 'rules' to the above apply here also, except that the boxer is side facing.

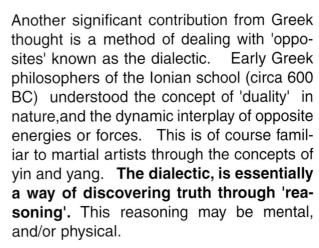

---

*Any movement change by the oppo-
nent is seen through the Lama 'gun-
sight' guard hand, placed opposite
his midline.*

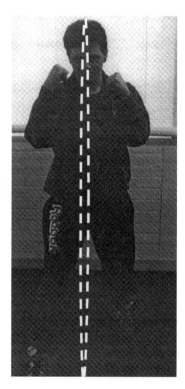

The Greek word Logos meaning word(s), is
the root term for 'logic' and implies a reasoning through words, say for example debate.
Indeed this was the dialectical style adopted
by Socrates, and his pupil Plato (5th century
BC).   Socrates was fond of challenging people who made claims to knowledge, to show
how it was that they knew what they held to be
true.   He said that to discover 'truth' it did not
matter if you started in error, provided that
your intention was earnest, and honest
enough, then, truth would 'emerge'. In effect,
this was intellectual pressure testing!
However, it is a sad truth that many of today's
leading western martial arts commentators,
far from embodying the spirit of Socrates,
have in fact no understanding at all of their
Greek heritage, and even go so far as to
decry logic and reasoning as being in some
way sinful, or otherwise easily dispensed with,
usually in favour of 'tacked-on' eastern meta-
physical ideas, couched in little more than an
agreeable quality of 'feeling'.

Another, later development of the dialectic
method, proposed that life was driven by

*The same as above applies
whatever posture the
opponent assumes.*

For more than one attacker, spread around, the attention is directed to their feet as the first indicators of movement and direction of possible attack.

complementary opponent (opposite) processes; that these eventually transcend each other by resolving into a new position. This was held to be equally true for ideas (theories) and for actions (physical processes).

Hop Gar Mantis Syncretism

Hop-Gar Mantis Kung-Fu is a syncretism existing physically between two oriental martial arts systems; and philosophically between the best and most relevant aspects of both eastern and western culture. This has been achieved 'dialectically' by psychological and physical 'pressure testing', a truly cosmopolitan Kung-Fu system.

The principles and applications presented in this book will be formatted to allow an on-going dialectic to emerge at relevant points, so the reader can see how different perspectives, both eastern and western, can add to the overall picture. Sometimes, a synthesis position will be offered as a potential for overcoming the limitations or one-sidedness of either viewpoint. At other times, the reader is invited to generate his or her own analysis. Even at the level of concepts, pressure testing can be educational, and enlightening. 'Know Thyself!' was the advice of the Delphic Oracle in Greece and the philosopher Socrates.

Perception

Now let's look at the principles that make up the Hop-Gar Mantis System, starting with perception. **Perception here refers to the detection and understanding of a situation.** Detection can be taken in two forms: through the senses which psychologists refer to as 'data' driven, and indirectly through unconscious processing which is known as 'hypothesis' driven. Data driven perception relies entirely on what is recorded in any of the five physical senses (actually six to include the special sense of proprioception, that is, spatial positioning). Only what is 'in the senses', however limited, can be detected in this way. Hypothesis driven perception refers to the capacity of the brain to make guesses (hypotheses) about what is happening, either from the sensory data itself, or more usually from what is missing from the senses, but is actually probably there. **It is usual for us not to perceive everything accurately, so it can be useful for the sensory data to be 'second guessed' by the brain, in order to save on processing and reaction times, and even in the event of an attack, our lives!**

A lot of visual 'illusion' games work through the brain making guesses about what is really there, or not there, even going as far as 'over-riding' the senses. In such cases we are fooled by our automatic, unconscious guesses, as our senses in themselves are not fooled. They still 'see' what is there. **In the martial arts, accurate perception of a threat, and indeed a whole situation is vital.** In practice of course, martial artists have to live with hypothesis driven perception, like everyone else, and often it can be very useful. When it occurs, people will often say that they 'reacted instinctively'. However, it's more likely that they reacted according to a 'probability computation within the brain, drawing as much from models of earlier learned experiences as from instinctive reactions. Given that data and hypothesis driven detection occurs, what then of 'understanding'; how is this involved in perception?

'Understanding' is the end-process of perception, and provides context for meaning. Indeed, without appropriate context there can be no meaning at all. Simply put, it works like this. Something is detected through the senses. Anything incomplete in the sensory field is added to by the brain, on the basis of what is 'probably' there. Then, the brain draws on an appropriate context to make meaning of the situation. The whole process could be a sudden movement, caught in the periphery of the visual field (data); this movement is perhaps part of some sort of attack (hypothesis), then the brain makes meaning out of the situation by alerting a response, based on learning and conditioned reflexes (understanding).

Visual and body-feel cues in the traditional martial arts present us with the fact that perception is trained in a number of ways. Usually it is through visual or somato-sensory (body-feel) cues. Visual perception often involves training gaze and focus. For example in the Jook-Lum Mantis style, the gaze is centred (in front facing opponents), or around the lead shoulder (in side angled opponents). In Lion's Roar, the gaze is set along the mid-line of the body, or with the opponent's feet set around the periphery of the visual field as illustrated in the photographs.

Both of these make sense, in that the Mantis is primarily a 'close' fighting style, and the Lion's Roar was intended for use at a longer range and against multiple opponents. Training with weapons in Chinese systems usually calls for the student to 'follow' the weapon' for example a pole, with their eyes. The intention being to train the practitioner to be able to react to rapid changes of direction in their opponent's movements. Eye to eye gaze is sometimes recommended, but this is not usual. It's likely that this has arisen both for practical and for superstitious reasons. In a practical sense, fixed eye gaze is 'trance inducing' and so can actually slow reactions down. In a superstitious sense, all cultures have folk-beliefs about the eyes being the 'windows of the soul', and some instinctively employ eye-to-eye staring as a dominance or threat signal (as in all primate species). Others may find themselves dis-empowered as in the response, "He looked at me and I just couldn't hit him". Of course, once battle is joined, eye-to-eye gaze and/or focus is of little practical value, in that range and angles will be constantly shifting.

Signaling through facial expression is a different matter. Although 'visual' it need not mean direct eye-to-eye contact, and is a much more complicated system of communication. Indeed humans along with other primate species have evolved a most elaborate repertoire of expressive facial signals. They can be used to threaten cajole, deceive, just about anything. Experienced martial artists are aware of these signals consciously and can filter and manipulate their effects appropriately.

Other important visual cues from the face include 'blushing' and "blanching'. Of the two, blanching is the most dangerous (in straightforward cases), as this can signal an imminent attack. Further cues involve the assessment of ritual posturing, and threat or dominance displays, usually accompanied by verbal threats or animal-like guttural noises. Once again, the situation as a whole needs to be understood, which is a very complex process.

The other main form of perception is somato-sensory and proprioceptive. This feeling through the body, often referred to as sensitivity training, features in many martial arts. Some make much of the sensation of pressure and direction changes, detected through the forearms, and directed to and away from the mid-line of the body. Others opt for a 'whole body' sensitivity, which typically is related to grappling and ground-fighting. In both examples, perception still involves the same basic brain and psychological processes as outlined above.

Sometimes, the body-feel sensitivity is abstracted out, in an attempt to heighten awareness. This abstraction may involve the dampening down or total exclusion of the visual sense (e.g. blindfolding). This method is often portrayed as being 'more difficult' as the practitioners cannot see their partners' arms, for instance. However, in reality it is actually much easier than the inexperienced person might think. In practice it is very hard to restrict the visual field and the consequent reactions of the brain to just the forearm areas, as there is a just too rich a visual environment, and so therefore, a much higher chance of a distraction away from the task in hand! Staring away from a rapidly changing and close-in source of stimuli also allows a trance like altered state of consciousness to set in, clearing the brain of 'clutter' and allowing a degree of relaxed focus of attention, just as you get in hypnosis. If you watch such an exercise, you will find that experienced practitioners avert their gaze from their partner's arms, or even close their eyes for periods of time. This act is most likely unconscious at first, as the brain tries to minimise distracting visual cues. Later, practitioners acquire a learned response system, that automatically releases this behaviour at appropriate moments. Over time, this has become ritualised, and incorporated into the 'myth' of the systems in question. The result is an apparent belief that being blindfolded makes the exercise more difficult. This is not so, unless of course contact between the partners arms is broken off completely (so that no body-feel information is available) or, if the rules of engagement are broken, by the practitioners not following the variations on possible positions allowed for in the exercise.

Perception in Action

Grappling and ground-fighting sensitivity training covers a much more varied repertoire of responses than can be found in systems that may reduce body-feel training to forearm and centre-line positioning alone. Nevertheless, an understanding of the latter, if integrated into the overall training regimen, is extremely useful, as it trains 'contact reflexes' very efficiently. Sparring, and contact pressure testing, come closest to actual 'real' combat, and are probably the most efficient methods of training basic perception for the martial artist.

In the Hop-Gar Mantis system, perception training covers all the areas mentioned above. Jook-Lum Temple Mantis has many variations on arm-to-arm sensitivity training, and the Lion's Roar involves locking, grappling and ground-fighting, with the associated 'whole-body' sensitivity development arising from influences from Mongolian and Indian wrestling.

This principle of perception is vital to the martial artist. Training should be as realistic as possible, but also take into account the way the brain processes sensory information. Then, common perceptive errors can be compensated for, giving an edge over those who have not applied scientific knowledge to their practice. However, the application of science must not be allowed to negate traditional forms of sensory training, where these can be demonstrated to be efficient and purpose-

---

Bi-secting guard which cuts through the attacker's lead wrist and rear arm elbow, to attack the shoulders, off centre. This over rides centre line defences most effectively.

ful. **The main thing is to be open to the testing of concepts and traditional exercises, constructively.** Too often, where science is applied to the martial arts, it is used to 'de-bunk' or reject the older methods. The challenge for the scientific method is firstly to understand the 'art' and then to see if any contextual improvements can be made.

Abstracting perception as a combat principle makes no real sense, so, what comes next? Targeting! Targeting follows on naturally, from the perceptual processes of detection and understanding. Essentially it is the ability to sort the various sensory information, both data and hypothesis, into something useful which allows a cognitive (mental) map to form of the threat.

Targeting

This requirement ushers in the *'battle computer'*. Simply put, it works like a battle computer that identifies the

Similar to the above but this time cutting through the opponent's rear elbow and and rear arm wrist.

TORSO CLOCK

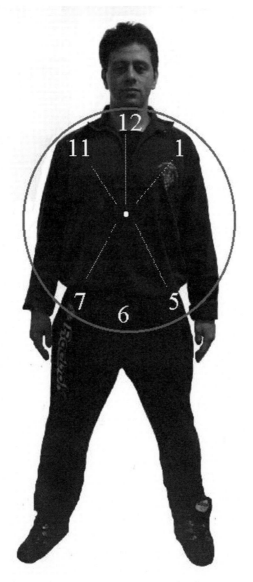

The 'torso clock' describes the major control points on the body, envisaged as a clock face. The solar-plexus, being the point from which all other points may be 'spot-located' as approximately equidistant. This allows for close-quarter control by 'mental imaging' as well as through 'direct feel'.

threat, its spatial location (position), movement and direction. Obviously, this cognitive mapping process needs to be fast and accurate. However, **speed and accuracy will go 'out of the window' if a person's training and experience just aren't up to it.**

Naturally, traditional martial arts styles have attempted all manner of ways to solve this particular problem. The more efficient ones have tried to develop a systematic approach, built around their basic techniques. The efficiency of this approach however, is limited by the techniques themselves. The less efficient techniques then 'contain' the reactions and responses of the practitioners, who may find at a cost that their system has trapped them into making outlandishly unreal responses, expressed through structurally slow techniques.

Then we must consider attack scenarios. The most efficient systems of all build their targeting responses not around techniques, but around a cognitive 'model' of attack scenarios. Given that most people are attacked by other people, the core model should be one that deals efficiently, quickly and accurately with the the human form. By 'form' I mean the actual morphological structure (shape) of a person.

All humans have the same fundamental form: a head, four limbs, and a torso. The simplest representation of this is the familiar 'pin man'. The possible range, and inclination of planes of movement, are actually fairly limited. As a problem, it is much less complicated to solve than many children's puzzles or games. Complications obviously include the use of weapons, multiple attackers and environmental variations, such as weather, time of day or night; and of course, space. Nevertheless, most of these factors can be accommodated if the basic cognitive model allows the battle computer to assess, plot, and respond appropriately.

Fighter Pilots

Research into combat cognitive mapping must then be considered. Cognitive mapping in combat was first researched by psychologists, during world war 2, when questions were asked about what the differences in information processing were, between ace fighter pilots, and all the rest. **It seems that the most successful pilots were able to 'second**

guess' their opponent's actions, both grossly, as in large movements over time, or very finely, through fractions of a second, say in the time taken for the target aircraft to alter course, so that it literally flew into fire.

When asked for their cognitive 'protocols' (their own understanding of what they were doing) by psychologists, **the fighter aces reported an ability to 'be the pilot of the enemy plane' and to understand the plane's shape and movement dynamics.** This act of 'being' the enemy pilot is an example of a tacit knowledge of human behaviour, the kind of things people just 'know', without need of any conscious thought; the appreciation of the aircraft's form signals understanding of what aircraft can do, simply by virtue of being aircraft.

The same factors are at work in martial arts combat. In effect the most efficient systems will utilise the simplest form of cognitive mapping, which will then provide context for techniques. It's quite easy to see how the reverse of this, the use of techniques to determine mapping, would be disastrous in air-to-air combat!

Human Form Modelling

The cognitive modelling of the human form can be helped by the 'pin man' as a simple cognitive map. This was impressed heavily upon me, when I witnessed a demonstration by scientists studying the psychology of perception, in 1982. In a pitch black room, two human figures, dressed totally in black, blended into the darkness and became of course, completely invisible. However, suddenly, tiny lights appeared, moving about in a chaotic way. It wasn't at all clear what was going on at first, until suddenly they stopped moving. At that point, although the people still could not be seen, what was clear was the impression of two human figures! The only visual information the audience had was a series of twelve lights, but they seemed by their pattern to suggest human form. The lecturer pointed out how little information was actually needed, by the brain, in order to make sense of a pattern, in this case the form of a human outline. The lights were arranged one on each wrist, elbow and shoulder, and one on each ankle, knee and hip.
What immediately struck me was the similarity between this 'illusion' and a sensory training method employed in Jook-Lum Temple Mantis. The

LIMB CONTROL POINTS

These refer to control points sited on the major joint articulations of the limbs. Control of these points allows control of the opponents offensive and defensive movements. They also lie close to vital and pressure control points. Remember, that however the arms are positioned, the head is *always located* at the end of them: the same is true for the legs, the groin; (torso clock number 6) is always at their end points (number 3) no matter how positioned. This allows for 'blind' target location by 'feel'.

Mantis considers that there are three control points on the arm: the wrist, the elbow and the shoulder. All hand and arm movement in any plane are articulated through these locations; that is the joints. Therefore, the Mantis boxer, during sensitivity training, seeks contact and control of them.

Wing Chun Comparisons

Comparisons with Wing-Chun Kung-Fu are helpful. I have been very fortunate to have studied the excellent Wing-Chun system, firstly with Kenneth Liu (as a student of Joseph Cheng in1973) then with Franco Chun of Macao 1975-1977, and currently under Master Samuel Kwok the senior student of Grand-Masters' Yip-Chun and Yip Ching. There are many similarities between the Mantis and Wing-Chun systems, as well as some intriguing differences. Some of these differences (more of emphasis than detail) concern theories of contact and control on the opponent's arms. In the Mantis, every effort is made to obtain control of the adversary's arm above the elbow and preferably, at the shoulder. Once the shoulder is reached the game should end quickly, as the head and neck are only inches away. In Wing-Chun the emphasis appears to focus between the wrist and elbow, effectively, on the forearms. Pressure changes are certainly felt through all three joints: witness the bong, tan and fook-sau movements. But in inexperienced practitioners, little attempt seems to be made to pass higher up the arm. I believe that this is due to the Wing-Chun centre-line approach contrasted with the Mantis emphasis on bisecting or 'x-ing' the centre line(see figures). Both are extremely functional, and indeed complement one another very well. It would be productive of students of these two styles to exchange views and learn constructively from one another.

Developing the tradition, the Mantis school refer to their understanding of this as the 'sam gwan' or three points theory. However, what really inspired me was the obvious implication that the sam gwan principle could be extended to the legs as well as the arms. This led me to explore what further insights might be gained from an analysis of the 'pin man'. Having had my eyes opened, so to speak,it didn't take long to 'reason' out the next steps.

It was clear that the brain required very little information in order to make sense of either detected movements, static postures, or changes between the two. However, it might be necessary to train the brain to react in this simple way, as the sensory environment of combat is very rich, and is heightened by the effects of stress hormones, and distracting thoughts.

Targets

Targeting should simply involve picking out the overall 'shape' of an attack, in time (movement), and, being sufficiently trained in a practical, experiential sense, to be able to engage, control/divert its path. So far so good. However, the implicit assumption in this might be that there is range (distance) involved prior to the attack. What if immediate contact is involved, with the body? How could you 'see' things outside of your visual field? Clearly the principle needed further development. Taking the 'contact' perception of the Mantis sam gwan as a starting point, I began to consider how it might be possible to point-map the parts of the body that aren't limbs, and to spot-locate any weak point on the body. **My answer was to introduce, and later pressure test, the concepts of the body (torso) clock, and the control planes.**

The body clock extends the sam gwan by envisaging the human torso as a clock face, with the solar plexus being the point at which the clock hands are placed. From the solar plexus, all the following points are roughly equidistant. The shoulders, the throat, the hips, and the groin. Each was assigned a clock-face number: right shoulder 11 o'clock, the throat 12 o'clock, left shoulder 1 o'clock, left hip 5 o'clock, groin 6 o'clock, right hip 7 o' clock. Obviously, the head should be considered a fifth limb, in that it articulates through joints at the top of the torso clock, and that it is routinely used as a weapon, as in butting.

This suggested that there were three upper limbs, at the top of the clock, and two lower ones at the bottom. The sam gwan on both the arms and legs, together with the body clock, gave 'source of movement control referents'. Any point or points on either the torso, or the limbs (including in this special sense the head and neck) can be topographically (spatially) located, by their relative distance from the control referents.

TRANSVERSE CONTROL PLANES

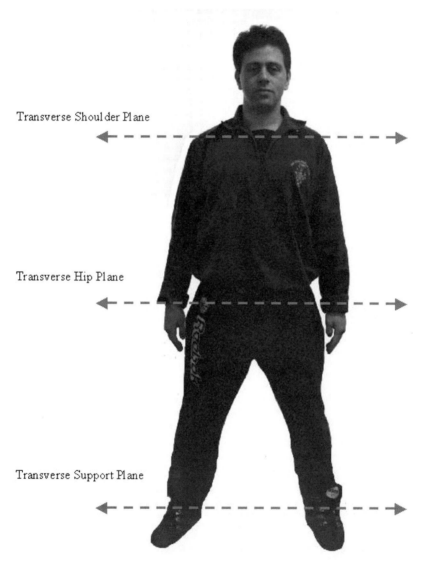

Transverse Shoulder Plane

Transverse Hip Plane

Transverse Support Plane

The 'transverse' or horizontal control planes allow either an upright or or 'ground-fighting' control of the major joints of the body (see torso-clock). The head should be considered as a 5th limb lying along the shoulder plane. Control of the hips is effectively control of the legs. The support plane describes the 'stance' and power-base of the opponent.

MEDIAN CONTROL PLANE

This describes the famous 'centre-line' commonly addressed by many martial arts systems. Along this axis (plane) lies the bodies centre of gravity and balance. Your object should be to 'knock' this plane out of alignment with the body. Your opponent *must* then fall in the direction that the plane is moving.

However, something else needed to be added; this was provided by the theory of control planes. The theory envisages four control planes, as a good, functional minimum. It would be entirely possible to introduce more, but this would contradict the overall parsimonious or meanly simplifying approach, and would unnecessarily complicate what I call targeting computation.

The control planes consist of three horizontal/transverse (crossing the body and parallel to the ground), and one vertical (90 degrees perpendicular to the ground). The first is generally referred to as the shoulder plane. Anatomically, this runs horizontally, across the body, from the 'acromion process', of one shoulder, to the other, and passing through the 'sterno-clavicular notch'. The acromion process is the bony prominence at the anterior (front) of the shoulder joint, formed by the articulation of the scapula (shoulder blade) and the clavicle (collar bone). The sterno-clavicular notch is the cavity at the top of the sternum (breast bone), between its articulations with the clavicles.

Essentially, this takes in points 11, 12, and 1, on the body clock, which are source of movement referents for both shoulders, and the head. The second control plane is referred to as the hip plane. Anatomically, this runs horizontally, across the body, from one neck of femur (thigh bone) to the other, encompassing both hips (including the iliac crests), the groin and the tan tien point (the 'Golden Stove' of chi-gung). This takes in points 5, 6 and 7, on the body clock.

The third control plane is the support plane. This refers to the relative position and contact of the feet with the ground. Effectively then, this describes the stance taken by the target. Obviously, a broad support plane in defined by widely spaced feet, and a narrow one by feet placed closely together. Standing on one foot is the narrowest possible support plane. If the target is 'airborne' so to speak, then there is no 'support plane' for the period of time that there is no upright contact with the ground. A target that is lying on the floor also has no support plane as such. In this case, the three planes are still considered, as the hip plane can isolate and control the feet, 'remotely'. Also, the sam gwan on the legs may be used to control strike or destroy, hips, knees or feet. On the ground, the upper plane can be manipulated to isolate action from the hips and feet, dependent on the relative positions of attacker and defender.

The last control plane is known anatomically as the median plane. It is familiar to martial artists as the 'centre line', and runs down the centre of the body from the top of the head to the floor. It is also known as the 'balance plane', because the centre of gravity of the body lies along its axis, when standing upright in a 'natural stance'.

This plane passes downwards through points 12 and 6 of the body clock, taking in the solar plexus, as the central referent point of the body clock. Remember from this point all control points on the torso are the same distance away. In effect, if you locate the solar plexus, you can 'find' any other clock point with ease, as well as any vital point associated either with major organs, nerve plexus, joints, cavities, or muscle-bone attachments, and so on. This 'finding' need not be with the hands; it can be with the body, or specifically through your own planes, and control points, including the median or centre plane. Sensitivity to your own shifts in balance and centre of gravity is a form of sensing, related to 'proprioception' the awareness of the relative position of limbs, and the torso, in space This is especially useful in grappling, ground-fighting and 'seeing without looking' (in a visual sense). In other words a 'whole body' sensitivity. Without doubt, this trained ability to sense with the whole body is due to the development of a cognitive, combat map, and, its application will give the impression of great speed and versatility in the practitioner.

Limbs as Reference Points

The limbs are very useful referents in themselves. No matter how an attacker's arm is positioned relative to you, his head is always at the end of it, at the 'end of its line' so to speak. The same is true of the groin and tan tien, they are always at the 'beginning' of the leg(s) no matter how they are positioned, or are moving.

'Balance breaking', as a fundamental attack strategy, often targets the control points and planes on the opponent's body. With respect to the centre of gravity, **Hop-Gar Mantis encourages its practitioners to**

visualise punching or kicking the centre of gravity out of the target, as the opponent's body must then fall towards it.

When making target computations, the 'battle computer' must sift and sort the changing status of incoming, and hypothesised information, rapidly. Obviously, errors will occur, but if the internal mental model is sufficiently simple and flexible, mistakes will be minimised, and many of those that do occur can then be corrected, with no appreciable break in the rhythm of movement. So, once the basic format of the body clock, and control planes, have been transferred to the 'pin man', it is a relatively simple matter to deal with changes in target orientation, such as variations in posture and angles of attack.

The body clock and control planes are quite distinct from the traditional Chinese martial arts perspective on the division of the body into areas. Usually, this involves four segments, known as gates, divided vertically by the centre line and horizontally by a line either through the solar plexus, or the tan tien.   Practical pressure testing, and conceptual analysis, between the two, has caused me to firmly favour the body clock system. In my experience it works better in actual combat, and communicates more simply and directly to students.   The body-clock and control planes system was actually approved of, as a new development, by Jook-Lum Temple Mantis Grandmaster Lee-Sun-Wah. Of course, these developments are based upon my own experience and as before, I invite readers to explore the issues themselves, in order to come to their own judgement and understanding.

Range for Combat

Now, given perception and targeting principles, what comes next? Range! A confused terminology: 'Range' as a concept has received a lot of attention in the theory of the martial arts. Currently, it is fashionable to sub-divide combat range under four headings: kicking range, boxing range, trapping range, and grappling range.   A major difficulty here is the confusion between 'range' which is a variable of distance, and groupings of techniques, which in themselves are not ranges at all! This issue of classification is actually quite a serious one, as it clearly implies some rather 'woolly' thinking underlying the division of range into techniques, a so-called category error, in western philosophy. The conscious understanding and articulation of concepts largely rests on the correct use of words; otherwise the foundations of our understanding becomes shaky. This isn't merely about semantics, as they are popularly understood, it's actually about 'meaning' and therefore knowledge.

Proponents of these technique-to-range classifications also usually make use of the term entry technique to describe the act of making contact with their opponents. These terms are now so widely, and uncritically accepted, that often, interpretations of just about any martial art, or street fighting situation, are routinely made by reference to them. Some martial artists, even from those schools known for introducing and developing these ideas, have noted the difficulties inherent in what otherwise may become a dogma, and pointed out that rigid range classifications have no absolute validity, at all. **Conceptual systems that imply such neat classifications eventually generate serious contradictions in themselves, as practitioners struggle to make the facts fit the theories.**

In Hop-Gar Mantis, the topic of range is reduced, as a starting point, to its most elementary factors: contact and non-contact. This is the simplest position from which to consider all possible variations on range. As an example, in concert with Chinese tradition, the Hop-Gar element of the Combined Style is generally held to be a 'long-hand' and the Mantis element a 'short hand', system. These terms are as we shall see, although generally accepted, in fact quite misleading. However, if we accept the implication that Hop-Gar is a long-range style, and the Mantis a short-range style, what happens when they meet, by what criteria is range, as an interactive and relative variable, defined? After all, the Hop-Gar exponent may consider himself at 'long-range', whilst with equal validity, the Mantis boxer can consider himself at 'short range'. Which one is right?

From the Hop-Gar man's perspective, he may well be at long range, particularly if he has employed a destruction technique on his opponent's limb or limbs, at the extremities. On the other hand, the Mantis man may intercept the attack with a counter destruction technique on his opponent's attacking limb, also at the extremity. From the rigid dogma of range, based on the interpretation of a systems techniques, they are both right! Obviously, the range between them is the same, one person cannot be closer or further away from the other than he is to them.

To further develop this point, all experienced martial artists know that they can be kicked at any of the supposed 'four ranges' and that at 'kicking range' a kicking leg can be punched or even 'grappled'. In terms of the analysis of concepts, it is simply insufficient to claim that an objective classification of ranges into four neat categories is possible, and further, that any style may be placed meaningfully into one (or less likely more) of such ranges.

Bridges and Traps

To bridge or to trap?:The parsimonious Hop-Gar Mantis classification of contact/non-contact is actually supported by the traditional Chinese idea of the bridge i.e. the point of contact between fighters. This has been somewhat distorted in the 'pop' martial arts, by film representations of starting point, in tournaments, or in supposed real fights. The popularity of the 'crossed hand' position is often found in some serious martial artists too, particularly those who entertain the notion of 'trapping'.

Trapping, as it is commonly understood (or more likely misunderstood!), exists in all Chinese martial arts systems. However, in my own 33 years experience, I have only ever heard practitioners of one well known contemporary style hype-up the term 'trapping' in itself. In all other cases, what passes as trapping in the eyes of some is almost universally referred to as bridge work. This is a far more encompassing term, as the 'bridge' can be anything, and is never limited to wrist to wrist or forearm to forearm contact.

Range as opening-closing or varying:In the combined Hop-Gar Mantis style, beyond contact/non-contact, range is further conceived of as: opening, closing or varying. These terms may be contextualised as a range that is opening (increasing), closing (decreasing), or varying (interchanging), within either contact/non-contact, or, between contact and non-contact. Therefore, it is possible to increase, decrease or vary the range between attacker and defender, even when contact has established a 'bridge' of whatever form, just as it is possible to do so, before any contacting bridge has been joined. These minimal concepts reduce unnecessary 'clutter' in both perception and thinking, and can

An 'accelerated phoenix eye punch' inserted above the pelvic bone (iliac crest) to intercept an attempted kick at close range. Notice also the arm bridge performed simultaneously at point number 2 - elbow.

accommodate any combination of combative actions, such as: inter-ception, evasion, feinting, slipping, striking, grappling and so on.

Range is always placed within the over-riding principle of targeting so that the body-clock and control planes are overlaid on to the attacker, appropriately. So, having contextualised the principle of range, what comes next?

Rules of Engagement

'Engagement', in the Hop-Gar Mantis system, refers to 'working the bridge'. This does not mean a continuous state of 'sticking' to the oppo-nent, although it can and does include such techniques. Engagement also includes its apparent opposite, 'dis-engagement', and is contextu-alised within the principles of range, and overall targeting. Rapid engagement and disengagement on the opponent's bridge, are both valid, and may be part of a strategy of 'switching' the attack, from point to point. Where the range is open, and no contact has yet been made, there is in effect 'no engagement This notion draws on classical princi-ples from the Mantis system, which advises giving nothing away through 'posturing' or any kind of stance, until the last possible moment. It is summed up in the Mantis sayings:

'Start after the enemy, and arrive before them'.
'You don't come, I don't start'.

This helps to eliminate so called 'telegraphic' movements, but relies heavily on being able to plot, intercept, and destroy an attack. Telegraphic movements are most noticeable where attacks are direct and/or linear, provided of course that appropriate range, and reaction time is allowed for. Western fencing, with its predominantly side facing posture, straight leading movements, and lunging, skipping footwork, has developed strategies to detect telegraphic movements, but as in many oriental martial arts, these are artefacts created by their own tech-niques. **In other words, most systems implicitly train to fight them-selves!** Western boxing, with its very limited range of techniques, is also known for studying telegraphic deliveries. In this case though, round as well as straight lines are employed. The decisive factor is the limited variation available.   To overcome this predisposition to telegraphy, both of these western arts have produced highly developed feinting skills.

In the oriental based martial arts, many systems that rely on linear forearm to forearm contact, also study telegraphic movements, but again these are often merely artefacts, caused by the mechanical and conceptual structure of the systems in question. Typically, these systems have what are popularly known as entry techniques. This often sounds more impressive than it actually is, as in practice it can be a simple variation on a straight stepping lunge, with the opponent's lead hand grabbed or pulled away from the centre line, in order to land a single, or series of linear hand techniques.   Structurally, this kind of entry method, can be telegraphic in itself, and arises out of uncritical conceptual, and mechanical dogma.

Enmeshing

Enmeshing is a further term to be considered. Other Chinese styles, particularly those that favour long-arm or circumovements, such as Hop-Gar, tend towards a different approach to solve the problem of engagement.   Rather than stand still, and thinking in a simplistic and linear fashion, they tend to be mobile, like Western boxing and enmesh their movements with those of the opponent.   It is much harder to plot something that is continuously changing, in terms of distance, and at the same time offering a fluid reference point.

From the outside looking in so to speak **long-arm methods seem to be telegraphic,** as they involve large circular movements, sometimes following a full 360 degree arc.   However, on the receiving end, it is a lot less clear, as the complex patterns pass into and out from the viewer's visual field, at great speed and with overwhelming momentum.   Also, as actual contact is made, the arcs tighten considerably, and the speed increases, with attempts at blocking, utilised as pivots for switching attacks, or the blows themselves aimed at the blocking limbs, either to 'smash' them, or to strike at vital points. The concept here is to deliver **techniques that conceal actual attacks or responses, within an 'unplotable' pattern of complex movements.**   This is 'en-meshing', and as an interactive function, it hides its true intentions by mixing them within the attack or response patterns of the opponent. So, it is wise to re-consider some perhaps reflex judgements made about the speed and practicality of 'flowery' long-hand techniques. They might just take your head off!!!

The combined Hop-Gar Mantis style utilises the approaches of both parent systems to the principle of engagement. What is unique however is the application of the body clock, and control planes, once contact is made with the opponent's bridge. This application is independent of any consideration of long over short 'arm' techniques, or vice versa.

Worked Example

A worked example is as follows.   Imagine the interception of an opponent's right hook, with a 'cutting' right hand forearm block.   The block is in effect a simultaneous interception and strike, as it connects with the attacker's biceps tendon, which crosses the anatomically anterior aspect of the elbow joint (the second gwan on the arm).   This movement is supported by a synchronous leg trap against the attacker's leading foot, jamming both the ankle and knee points, and the covering of the wrist of the punching arm with the defender's left hand. The defender is positioned with his head to the outside of the attacker's arm, and has in effect 'slipped' the punch, as well as simultaneously blocked, jammed and 'trapped' the attacker.

This causes an immediate arrest of the attacker's momentum,   and chambers the defender for a number of counter-options.   These will be decided by the 'feel' of the situation, and any developing reactions in the attacker.   As a basic consideration, the battle computer may 'release'' any of the following:

(a) Carrying the force of the interception through the elbow joint, by hooking the arm over, and downwards, whilst sinking the body to push weight down into the attacker, simultaneously applying equal and opposite pressure to the ankle and knee joints of the attacker (breaking his stance), and following the line of the attacker's punching arm with a left forearm strike to the neck/throat (shoulder plane). This can then convert to a hooking arm to head lock combination for a take down and choke-out.

(b) Following the line of the engaged leg bridge, with a kick to the groin, and step-through on to the rear knee joint, with the defender's left arm, following the line of the attacker's right punching arm, directly to the neck/throat for a head lock, take down, and choke-out.

(c) from the interception at the biceps tendon, immediately strike with the edge of the hand to the throat, inviting a defensive 'slapping block' reaction. If the slap block comes, pivot round it to strike with an inverting single knuckle blow to the attacker's left carotid artery. As the pivot occurs, the defender's left hand can release its cover on the attackers right hand and 'receive' the now aimless slap block, by pulling it down, and across the attacker's right hand, effectively isolating the latter, by pinning it.

The 'bombardment' may (must!) continue, for example by converting the carotid strike to a downward scooping palm hit across the jaw, which converts again to a downward elbow strike, delivering 'sinking weight' power, into the sternum, and mid-line. The support plane is simultaneously compromised by a forward projection of weight from the defender, through the hips, and the knee and ankle joints, of the defender.

If the attacker throws a second left (rear hook) on being intercepted, this is easily stopped, by converting the intercepting cut to the elbow joint to a pivotal chop on to the attacker's left shoulder (1 o'clock on the body). Ideally, the blow should impact on to the acromio-clavicular joint, or directly on to the collar bone itself. The pivot must be 'relaxed' yet tight, and penetrate right through the shoulder. This gives excellent 'shock-stopping power'. The pivotal chop can then easily reach the neck, for a strike, or strike to head -lock to take-down combination. In principle, any number of variations are possible, and will be released according to circumstances.

A good stop-hit against counter kicks, particularly close hooks to the groin from an opponent in this initial position, whose lead leg has been engaged, is to strike at his right hip (7 o'clock), with a 'phoenix-eye' single knuckle hit (the extended middle knuckle of the index finger or the proximal interphalangeal joint). This should be delivered the instant any shift of weight is detected in the opponent that suggests through 'feel' that a kick is imminent. The strike should be 'inserted' above the iliac crest (bony prominence of the hip) on the kicking leg, and penetrate with follow through, and a simultaneous transfer of weigh downwards and through his shoulder plane, from your left hand. The effect is to crumple the attacker, by bending him in the middle, and causing excruciating pain. Further follow-ups should be at your pleasure!

Engagement then concerns contact with, and manipulation of, the opponent through a ''bridge' and focuses on the body clock points, and control planes. This will be discussed again later, and in more depth, under the principle of 'destruction'.

Speed

Let's now turn to the next principle, that of speed! **Speed as a concept, or principle, in the martial arts, suffers from a lot of misunderstandings, faulty premises, and dubious conclusions.** One of the most common, and most perpetrated errors, is to misapply the maxim that **the shortest distance between two points is a straight line! Whilst the statement in itself is true, it actually says nothing about speed at all, let alone acceleration, inertia or obstruction.**

The actual formula for speed is: speed (s) is equal to distance (d) over time (t).

$$s = d/t$$

In other words **speed is a function of the time taken to cover a given distance; it is not in itself described by the shape of a path, either linear or curved.** As an example, consider a person who is say ten miles from a certain town. He sets out on foot to walk in a straight line to that town. At the same moment his friend, on a motorcycle sets out from the same starting point, also intending to travel to the same destination. However, he goes by a circuitous route, of some fifty miles, and yet still arrives well before his ambulant friend.

Obvious isn't it !

Yet in the martial arts, there are still many people who, without thinking at all, dogmatically state that linear attacks are faster than circular ones. Yes, this is true, if the velocity over the two distances, described by the straight line and the arc, is the same, or if the velocity of the arc is slower.   However, it is false, if the velocity of the arc is sufficiently greater than that over the linear path. So much for elementary physics.   **What does psychology have to tell us about the perception and computation of speed?**

Speed and the psychology of perception may be considered next. In this context, I refer to the psychology of perception and as such it is related to the Hop-Gar Mantis principle, of the same name. **Speed in combat is as much about what is, or can be, perceived (detected) as it is about anything else.**   What you don't see, or implicitly account for, is more likely to hit you, however 'slow' it may be, objectively.   Also, changing speed conceived of as a rate of action can fool the best of us, particularly if we have been 'geared up' to react to a specific rate of 'fire'.

Martial artists can be geared up too quickly and even knocked out by a change of pace (speed) or a broken rhythm attack. So, speed must be used intelligently, not blindly.   Blind reliance on sheer velocity owes more to luck than skill, and whereas skill can be trained, luck is in the 'gift of the gods' and can therefore be revoked!

Speed is developed in a number of ways; firstly at a conceptual level, starting with a rebuttal of dogmatism about linear versus circular paths. Then an analysis of context for the choice of path, as context defines speed.   For example, the Mantis advocates contact with the bridge as closely as possible, hitting with the lead hand first, then striking at every available target (usually a vital point) in the manner of a machine gun.

Obviously this suggests speed.   However, it is only one kind of speed; that conferred by reducing distance.   In Hop-Gar, speed is conceived of as a product of overwhelming velocity and momentum, put together in bewildering combination attacks. As a 'sub-set' to this, speed of switching or re-direction of attack, by pivoting on the opponent's block or bridge

An incoming 'clubbing' strike to the point of the chin; fist in a semi-closed position. On impact, below, the fist closes into a 'squeeze' point giving more impact on the target; a good knockout blow.

is involved, usually so that the momentum of the attack is renewed.

I personally know of several people, some martial artists, and some street thugs, who were literally 'blown away' by the sheer velocity of Hop-Gar circular (but intelligently directed) attacks. Euphemistically, they were blown away by the Breath of the Buddha: the Lion's Roar! Some of the martial artists were dogmatic about straight lines. So much for dogma.

Timing

Timing is an essential ingredient for any consideration on speed, and one that need not be abstracted out from its living context. Physical training for speed is also important, and in both parent styles this is achieved by encouraging relaxation, and accuracy, whether over straight or round lines. Speed may also be conceived of as structural, by which I mean the potential for speed (and velocity) inherent in the structure of the techniques themselves.

Again I would say that structure without context is mere abstraction, and as an ideal context the combined style employs the body clock and control planes as the 'overlay' for its choice of techniques. **Speed then becomes what it really is, a relative factor, both quantitative (measurable) and qualitative (experiential).**

Power

Power is a further expression to be considered. In the combined style, power is considered as a mechanical, rather than as a mystical, function.   I say this in all seriousness, as many practitioners of traditional Chinese systems lose much of their credibility by waxing lyrical on 'internal' or mystical energy.

There is definitely a place for the practice of traditional exercises that purport to develop such power, but in my 26 years experience of Kung-Fu, and overall 33 years in the arts **I have yet to witness its actual application by a Chinese master, in a 'practical' situation.** By practical, I do not mean in the training school, or at demonstrations, or with suggestible 'volunteers', **I mean in a real fight, simple as that.** What I have seen is the very skilful use of body mechanics to deliver devastating force against an assailant.   Often, this involved the striking of anatomically vulnerable points on the body, but at other times it was simply Newtonian physics: the application of great force to a unit of body area.   **I stress the anatomical aspect, to separate my discussion from claims of 'meridian strikes' and so forth.** That which passes for such strikes will on proper scientific observation, be found to be on known anatomical weak points, and/or be delivered through the medium of considerable psychological 'suggestion'. Let no one underestimate the power of influence and expectation. It can kill!   More on these aspects below, under destruction and mental training, and Kung-Fu for the Street.

Shock Power

Shock power is our next subject. As we saw above, the Mantis compo-nent of the combined style employs what it refers to as **sudden shock, spring power.**   In practice, this refers to the mechanical use of the shoulder, and pectoral girdle muscles. Picture your arms as relaxed but extended car suspension springs, and shock absorbers. The waist is given free rotation, but the legs braced and the toes tensed as in grip-ping the floor. The extended shoulders (actually 'flexed' in correct anatomical terms),   increase 'reach' quite dramatically, by as much as 30 cm (12inches). The increased reach also provides greater penetra-tion through the target, and keeps your body further away from your opponent, by an equivalent distance to the extension of your arm. **This relaxed extension of the shoulder allows the generation of great power, not available in punching systems that 'lock' the shoulder back.**   Some variants of the Southern style family of Mantis systems, are quite stiff in the shoulder, even when it is extended.

I once demonstrated to a Chinese teacher the difference in power gen-eration, by use of a simple exercise: If you stand leaning against a wall, with bent elbows, and 'locked' shoulders, and then push forcibly for-wards, you will be able to 'feel' the power generated by the equal and opposite force passed back into your body. This is experienced as the force pushing you away from the wall. If you repeat the exercise, but this time with relaxed shoulders, the effect is magnified dramatically, demon-strating the huge increase in power generation.   After this, the Chinese Master in question was totally convinced, and actually modified his own practice accordingly.

Beginners, or other martial artists, unfamiliar with the mechanics of Mantis boxing, often fear that the increased arm extension, compromis-es stability of the shoulder joint, and is vulnerable to grappling. Actually, the arm extension is part of a whole package, which admittedly if it were abstracted as simple arm extension would be asking for trouble. However, it is delivered with such speed , and therefore momentum, that the follow through at close range (the Mantis's favoured distance) is phenomenal. Also, as the Mantis style prefers single knuckle impact points on nerves, blood vessels, joints, and muscles, the pain and tis-

---

Stances are both stable transitional platforms, from which to launch techniques, and also 'ramming and jamming' methods, used as weapons, in themselves...

sue damage involved is punitive. Further, Mantis attacks are rarely single 'big hits' but combined multi-level (simultaneous support, hip and shoulder plane engagements) bombardments. The systems skill at bridge work means that there is very little in the way of openings for the opponent's counter strikes. Of course, this is the theory as in 'the death of it', so to speak; it's down to individual people and situations, rather than the system in itself; although it is fair to say that some systems do confer definite advantages over others.

Mantis Stance and Footwork

The Mantis stance and footwork for power generation are next. The other essential ingredient in the generation of power is the use of stance and footwork. The Mantis style appears to be relatively static, when the classical forms are viewed, yet this can be misleading; therefore it is important to appreciate why there is comparatively little movement in the system's forms. Firstly, a quick word about forms in general, although more will be added later. **Classical Kung-Fu formal exercises (routines) are in essence carriers of information, rather like biological genes,** although in this context they should be considered as 'cultural genes'. Just as in the case of the body's genes, the information carried in Kung-Fu forms is at best latent and at worst useless, if it is not 'read' properly. The value of forms is to pass information on to the next generation, which if correctly understood, can be translated into a bewildering variety of applications. However, blind, unknowing attempts to apply forms, out of context, are ineffective, and as such a waste of time.

Given that there is reasoning and potential in such forms, **how do we then make sense of the static postures, and limited stance movements found in the Mantis?**

Well, the Mantis is an intercepting system that employs a variety of destruction techniques. Its power derives from a sudden shock springing action, launched through relaxed shoulders, from a mobile waist, and 'rooting' power, from a braced, solid stance. Stances as such are not employed, unless the practitioner is 'doing something'. **In short, stances are stable artillery platforms, which may also be used to** attack the opponent's bridge, employ balance breaking actions, shift balance for kicking, jam the opponent's legs; provide support to 'receive energy', and to allow recoil from impact with the opponent, to bounce back into the floor, and thence back into the target once again.   Beyond these, they have no function! Therefore, in the traditional forms, you only see very limited footwork, but not the thinking behind them. Quite misleading, but then the Chinese masters are happy with this, as they don't 'give away' their secrets lightly!

Muscular Tension and Relaxation

Muscular tension and relaxation is an essential part of training. The training for shock power in the Mantis involves the drilling of very rapid cycles of tension and relaxation in the muscles.   This allows for explosive impact and speed.   The speed factor facilitates the lightning fast switching from one impact or control point to another, giving the impression as a 'victim' of being drilled or machine gunned.

Traditional exercises for power, in their basic form, consist of resistance exercises against a partner (usually through the limbs), but later involves the precise practice of forms, to develop the rapid tense-relax cycle. Various types of conditioning and strengthening exercises are also employed but these are considered as basic.   So called 'higher level' power is said to come from relaxation and speed, and at the most advanced levels of the Lee-Yin-Sing system, training exercises resemble those of Tai-Chi rather than hard, or 'external' styles.

Power training in Hop-Gar is quite different, mechanically, from the Mantis, in its generation and delivery of power, both in training and application to a 'target'. What it does have in common is the principle of 'relaxation', although in Hop-Gar this is more important as relaxation until the final squeeze point of contact is essential, due to the generally larger, and more circular movements.   Power in Hop-Gar is generated by maximal use of turning forces, starting in the twisting of the feet; then the waist, shoulders, forearm and wrist.   Like the Mantis, single knuckle fists are routinely employed, in order to increase the end point delivery of power to the target.

The squeeze point focus of tension on impact produces an effect which traditionalists refer to metaphorically as being like hit by a cannon ball on the end of a chain. At the instant of impact, the body and striking point become tense, and thereby impart terrific momentum into the target.

Like the Mantis, Hop-Gar stylists employ pivoting and 'switching' as a way of by-passing blocks or interceptions. In the Hop-Gar style however, this is often a change of height, relative to the opponent, whereas in the Mantis, the switch tends to be in and around the engaged bridge.

Stance and leg manoeuvres in Hop-Gar are far more varied and mobile than in the Mantis. The full range of stances typically found in northern Chinese systems are incorporated. Kicking techniques however reveal a mixture of those found in northern and southern styles. The use of stances to generate power in Hop-Gar relies on the torque generated by full body twisting, and the triangulation of focused force into the target. In the traditional style, the principles of chune (penetrate) and chon (destroy), impart an aggressive intention. The stances and associated footwork are therefore delivery systems for penetrative and destroying power.

Another aspect of Hop-Gar power is the use of shuffle and jump stepping techniques, for 'dropping' body weight into the target; usually this is done through the interception of the opponent's attack. The jumps and shuffle steps allow contact with opponent's legs and arms, simultaneously breaking balance and dropping mass and momentum into the attacker.

Power training in Hop-Gar follows the parallel tracks of drilling for the stamina necessary to employ its fast flowing long-arm techniques, and, the relaxation necessary for speed, with the training of squeeze point focusing on impact. Some of the most powerful punching techniques I have ever seen derive from Hop-Gar.

The 'J' Punch

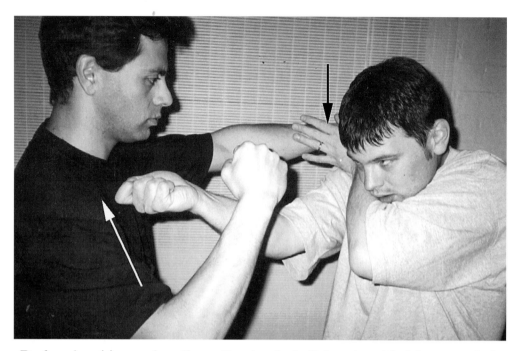

Defender (r) parries the attacker's left hook with his own left hand, covering his chin in the fold of his arm, and striking the attacker's right shoulder joint with a phoenix eye fist destruction hit. This hinders a right hook attack by his opponent and gives the defender the possibility of hitting to the neck with his left hand as a follow up.

One of the most unusual is nicknamed the 'J' punch, after the shape of the punching arc itself. This punch starts like a western boxer's hook, but impacts like a twisting uppercut, with full body torque and twisting on the stance. It can be delivered from an upright position, or as a jumping/shuffling technique. A number of derivations are employed including a jumping uppercut, and a block-breaking hammer blow.

Nevertheless, the traditional viewpoints on power generation and delivery are only at one level of description and explanation. Western science, in the form of kinesiology and sports and exercise science, is quite capable of describing, understanding and reproducing the power poten-

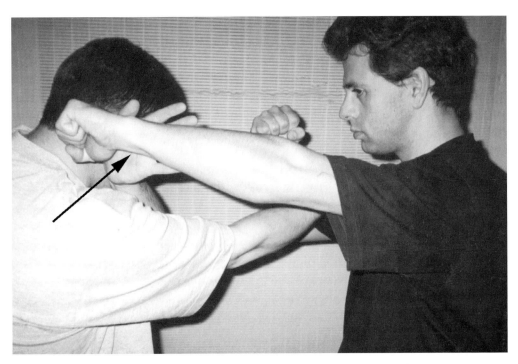

Same technique as on the previous page, seen from the other side, to emphasise arm and hand positions.

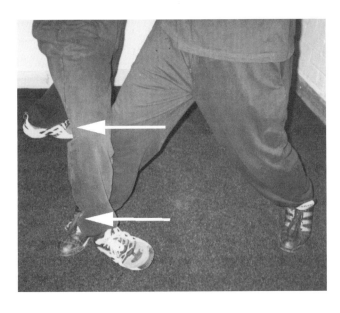

Exemplary and typical leg/stance ramming attack which should accompany all arm bridge engagements, in general.

Thus the opponent is affected at the opposite 'poles' of his body, simultaneously.

tials in the Mantis Hop-Gar, and indeed any other system, without recourse to arcane or esoteric beliefs, and terminology.

To summarise, the two parent systems of the combined Hop-Gar Mantis style, although different in many ways, function together in a complementary and compensatory way, to generate a devastating power delivery system. The combined Hop-Gar Mantis style synthesises the best

A single arm multiple strike sequence: straight finger thrust to the brachial nerve plexus, deep and behind the collar bone...

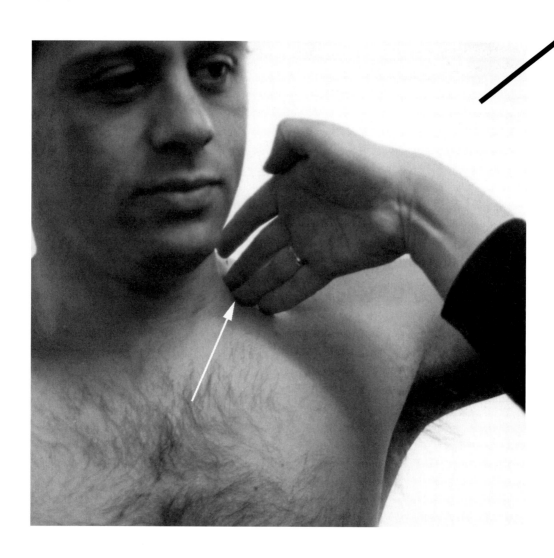

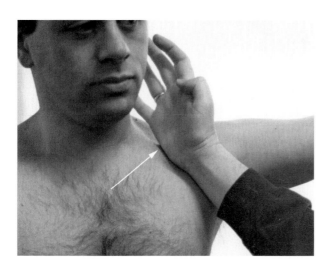

leading to a chopping action to the clavicle or collar bone...

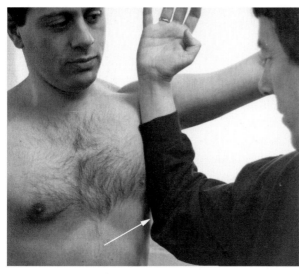

finally an elbow/forearm strike to the chest.

of the two into an empirically tested method. Therefore western science and eastern tradition offer alternative but by no means mutually exclusive methods for modelling, training, and improving the practitioner's development, and delivery of power.

So what do we do with all this power? Destruction!

Tibetan and Chinese Derivations

Tibetan and Chinese derivations in the combined Hop-Gar Mantis system use the principle of destruction based on traditional principles. These concern vital point attacks on the head, torso, and limbs, as well as balance breaking interceptions and strikes. The popularisation of the term 'destruction' is due mainly to the efforts of Filipino and Indonesian stylists, particularly from the Kali and Silat schools. However, the use of such techniques is also an established feature of many Chinese and Tibetan systems, and indeed has been so for many centuries. For example, **in the Tibetan Lion's Roar, there are five core principles for combat:** Chon (destroy) Chune (penetrate) Jeet (intercept) Sim (evasion) Lin (continuation). In the Jook-Lum temple Mantis all the style's so-called speciality hands (e.g. single knuckle fist formations) are used to strike (destroy) anatomically vital points, on the target. In both systems, destruction techniques are considered as fundamental. By this, I mean neither basic nor advanced, but rather as part of the 'essence' of their practice.

The refinement of skill is an essential feature of martial arts development. Amongst the many theoretical and practical tensions current in the martial arts is that arising from the debate between practitioners who mainly favour the development of technical skill, and those who are in the main athletes, favouring fitness, strength and aggression. There is no doubt merit in both of these polarised positions, but from the perspective of destruction techniques, the right balance between the two is essential. Raw power has the tendency to be its own self-justification. It has probably always been so since the earliest times in the evolution of the human species, and may still be seen today in ritualised dominance behaviour, both in humans and in our nearest primate relatives, such as baboons and chimpanzees. One of the factors that makes us human is the refinement of skills, of any kind, including of course combat-power skills.

The modelling of combative systems supposedly on the characteristics of animals is a well known feature of Chinese martial arts. The Lion's Roar(Hop-Gar) style purports to be an amalgamation of ape and crane techniques, and of course, the Praying Mantis system takes its origin from the form and spirit of that particular insect.

The Hop-Gar ape techniques tend to be circular, almost 'clubbing' in nature, whilst the crane movements are more specialised, even 'stylised'. However, the ape movements, in application, are used intelligently, with their momentum often used to strike at very specific vital points. Thus they are far from being wild swings, and are certainly not just the use of brute force in preference to skilled technique. The Mantis is a more obviously refined system, with shorter, smaller and precise, pin-point needle like strikes and interceptions.

Vital Points Attacks

The combat application of refined vital point skills takes time to develop, and few modern day martial arts students have the necessary time or motivation to learn effectively. Naturally, this leaves the door open to some kind of compensatory development; one that takes less time, effort and perhaps intelligence. Where all else fails (or seems impractical), basic aggression and brute force, with minimal technique, appear to be the better option.

It has often been said that vital-point skills are 'unrealistic' in a real street encounter. This is untrue. In my thirteen years' practical experience as a Liverpool Police Officer, **the use of vital point and destruction techniques have probably saved my life, and on many other occasions saved me from a severe beating.** I should of course emphasise that I am not referring to the use of mystical techniques or 'chi', but to the pressure testing of refined skills and economical force. If the martial arts are to be about anything on a physical level, then they should be about the ongoing development of refined skills. This is art or a craft as in the craft of an artisan. It is not athletic prowess as such, or even aggression. We can get 'fit' in any number of ways without being martial artists, and aggression can be safely ventilated elsewhere, without working-out on weaker or more emotionally vulnerable people. Therefore, if one of the higher physical attributes of the martial artist is the acquisition of refined skills, then the perfection of vital point and destruction techniques must stand at the very pinnacle of achievement.
Destruction needs to be contextualised within the larger picture provided by the other guiding principles. In effect, it is the end-

point or goal of all those preceding principles. This is known in Greek philosophy as 'teleology' or the doctrine of the final cause, i.e. that which was present in a latent but causative sense, even at the beginning of the process. In other words, all combative actions and causes have their fulfilment in the 'destruction' of the opponent's attack.

This deceptively simple idea draws together the elements of perception of a threat; its targeting and range; its engagement with speed and power , which then leads to its destruction. **All of the combined style's principles therefore work in concert to achieve this final goal.**

Coming to more specifics, destruction in its narrower sense refers of course to the striking of anatomically vulnerable points on the body, but it also applies to the function of balance breaking. Any strike can compromise balance, and notwithstanding direct head shots, ones which are aimed at control points on the body clock, and limbs, are particularly effective. Pain also supplies an objective major focus of attention, which then becomes a balance breaker in its own right. A powerful impact in the general area of a torso clock control point can be extremely painful, even if not a direct hit on a pressure point. As an example, consider the shoulder. The shoulder is 'off-centre' with respect to the mid-line, and so is often disregarded as a target by styles that may dogmatically address centre line to centre line techniques; yet, the shoulder is the power joint for punching attacks, particularly hooks.

Traditional martial artists are not particularly well known for their technical ability in dealing with expertly delivered round-line attacks, hence their vulnerability to western boxing. The usual answer is to mimic boxers, probably in the belief that if 'you can't beat 'em, copy 'em'. However, there is another way. As an exercise, simply to build up confidence in developing your destructive stopping power, get a training partner to throw a determined right hook, straight at your chin, launched from about one-and-a half times your own arm's length away. This is close enough for you to see the attack develop, and to be intimidated by it! In response, step straight forwards from a natural stance with your hands down by your sides, and deliver a straight right cross punch to your partner's shoulder.   Don't pull your punch, but you will find that you actually need comparatively less impact force to stop the attack.

If delivered correctly, your partner should be stunned, perhaps with a slight whiplash injury to his neck, as the impact force of his own punch, and your interception, recoil back through his body, and, through the nearest major joint articulation to the shoulder; that is, to the neck.

So much for playing, now to gear up a bit!   If he's still your mate, ask him to come in again, this time, relax, and go for speed, and follow through. With your hands by your sides, you can 'draw and fire' your destroying counter-punch, non telegraphically, like a western gun-fighter.   Your punch should be a 'cross' (i.e. crossing your centre-line to the opposite side), as this gives greater triangulation of force. Don't be put off by people saying that this exposes you to counter attacks, the impact or even the 'placing' of your fist on your partner's shoulder, places you inches from his neck and head, and additionally, allows pivotal re-direction, from a fixed elbow, to strike at the opposite shoulder (or elbow joint against a wider arc counter) should a second hook follow.   This works against feints as well,   insofar as your 'battle-computer' simply incorporates the error, by switching to an anticipatory strike at the opposite shoulder, perhaps taking the chin or throat out, by horizontally moving along the shoulder plane, from your left to your right.

As a final development of this very basic exercise, ask your now wary partner to 'pad-up' appropriately with protective equipment. Then to throw a third hook attack.   This time, you should step forward with a 'stomping' action, twisting your waist and feet,   and project your punching arm forward to its maximum reach (by not locking the shoulder) and aim to follow through on impact, by as much as 12 to 18 inches.   Also, land your punch 'palm up', with a single index finger knuckle fist formation (Phoenix eye) impacting against the joint between the clavicle (collar bone) and the scapula (shoulder blade): the bony lump at the top and front of the shoulder. This devastating, yet simple blow, can finish a fight all on its own.   In effect, you have here a worked example of a combined vital point and balance breaking, destruction technique.   It can easily break an opponent's shoulder joint, causing

Impact against the sternum with a ginger fist strike.

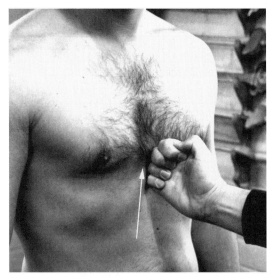

great shock and pain, and yet you haven't even started to develop your ongoing counter attack, which can finish with single knuckle strikes to the carotid or windpipe; headlock-take down and choke-outs, or whatever.

Some martial arts systems, counsel 'rolling with the blow' if a strike comes at the shoulder, saying this dissipates attacking force. Usually, they then go on to say that centre-line attacks cannot be avoided, as they will always find their mark. To test the practicality of this, ask your partner to 'roll with the blow'. You should notice how this actually turns his centre-line towards your punching arm, and in particular, exposes his throat and neck, which are now much closer to you (and therefore available for grabs, strikes etc.) even than they were before. As for centre-line attacks always finding their mark, this obviously depends on the relative mobil-

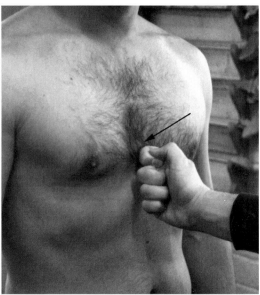

Contact hit as an accelerated' phoenix eye' strike.

ity and elevation (height) of the opponent, to your centre-line attack. It ' will work if both stand relatively still, or only rotate around their mid-line, in an otherwise static posture. However, change the variables, and the dogma merely disappoints (perhaps disastrously so).

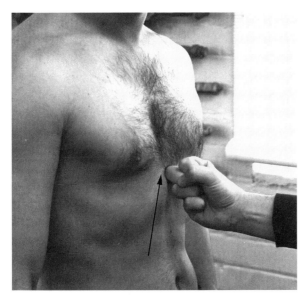

Initial impact with a 'chicken heart' knuckle fist to the solar plexus, followed by a contact accelerated 'phoenix eye' knuckle strike.

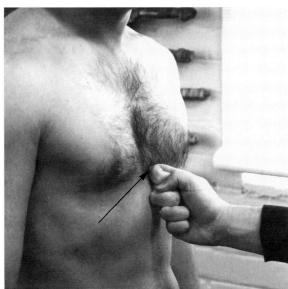

Again, I invite readers to empirically test these ideas, without submission to either dogma or 'suggestion'. Compliance allows the survival of many woolly concepts in the martial arts. A scientific approach to 'testing' styles and techniques is one of the most beneficial contributions the west can make to the further development of eastern martial arts systems. It's good for your personal survival too!

Multiple Strikes

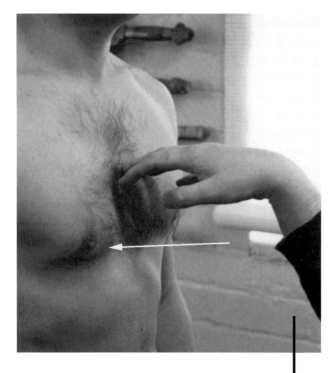

Collapsing palm strike to the heart, showing relative distance to the shoulder and torso clock control points :

11, 12 and 1 o'clock.

Multiple strikes may be considered next. The above worked example, provides an introductory exercise for learning applied destruction techniques. More advanced skills involve the simultaneous engagement, control and striking, of points at different levels of the body; and/or the delivery of rapid-fire multiple hits, to points on a single limb, or body area. Naturally, these require more experience and skill, but they can be made easier if the right approach is taken.

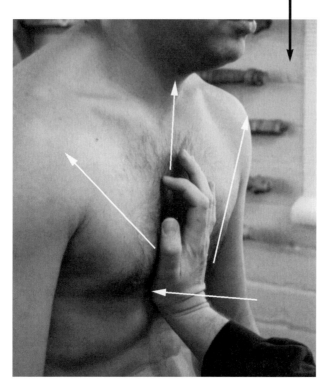

In applied destruction techniques, there are three factors which separate the advanced exponent from the beginner. Firstly, of course, there is the basic knowledge

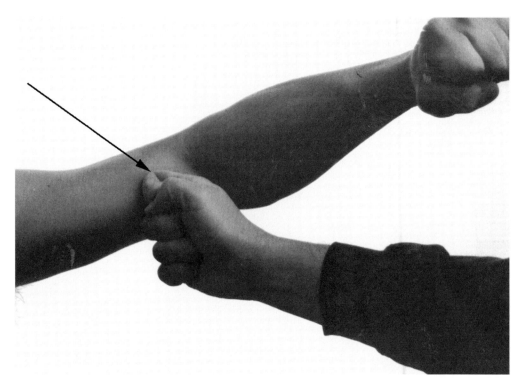

"Shooting down" a hook punch with a phoenix eye hit.

required to point-map vital and control areas.   Secondly, the economical use of angles and distance and thirdly, proper technique itself.

The first is best studied under the guidance of an experienced teacher, but this must be supplemented by your own continuing self-education. In part from exploration with yourself and with a training partner, and in part from a study of relevant scientific anatomy and physiology.   There is a case for the study of traditional point-mapping, as in the Chinese discipline of dim mak but some caution needs to be exercised in this.

With respect to angles and distance, **advanced exponents often seem to be so very fast, because they are economical not only in energy, but also in regard to the quickest angles, and the most appropriate distancing.**   For example, many beginning practitioners 'forget' their lead or contacting hand, and try to hit from the rear hand.   Often the experienced fighter, will hit with an accelerated knuckle hit from the

Phoenix eye punch delivered to the eye.

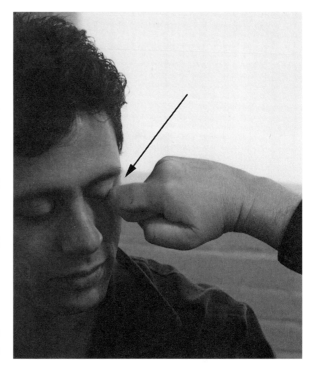

lead hand, directly into a vital point, which is only inches away from the strike's starting position (e.g. shoulder to carotid). At other times the use of small angles can stop an opponent, merely by a slight inclination or turn of the wrist, delivering a knuckle hit into a new target.

In the board game of Chess, there is the idea of a so-called 'passed pawn'. The passed pawn is a humble chess piece which has been advanced so far that it is now positioned deep into the opponent's board space. On its own, a pawn is generally of little threat to the overall game. However, in a 'passed' position, it can suddenly strike or control directly the heart of the opponent, or be used as a support for a further attack. **The 'passed hand' is just the same;** it can be deadly.

Another error made by beginners is to 'arc-off', which means to turn off-plane, with respect to the opponent. For example, consider the opponent's shoulder plane. As a 'thought experiment' think of this plane to be a straight horizontal line. If you control this plane, you will prevent movement by either shoulder (or arm) and the head (preventing butting or biting). The most effective way to do this is to 'bar' along the entire length of the plane, from shoulder to shoulder. In an actual fight, opportunities for this will occur, the main thing is not to lose contact with the plane. If you 'push' with your bar too much against say the opponent's left shoulder, a gap of a few inches will open against his right. These few inches, at the shoulder, can give him about 12 inches extra

Light contact thrusting attack to the eye. Note the controlling action of attacker's (r) left hand above defender's elbow. Also the positioning of his attacking elbow on top of the defender's leading bridge, which is also at the elbow joint.

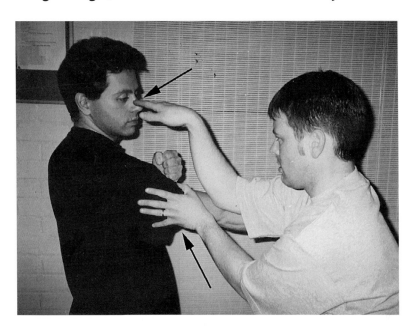

reach at the fist end of his arm!   The consequence of this can easily be imagined.

Now, applying this same idea of arcing-off to any contact engagement, it is easy to see how all manner of angles will close for you, and open for your opponent!   Therefore, the expert practitioner closes angles for his opponent and opens his own, exploiting each and every one of them in a punishing way. The angles are of course a function of knowledge of the body-clock and control points/planes and become the pathways for the delivery of the destruction techniques themselves. Destruction techniques can, at the end-point of their delivery, be in the form of any potential striking surface.   The more specialised tend to be what is known traditionally as speciality hands.   These are characteristic hand formations, often especially trained and conditioned for point-striking.

However,   end-point delivery is only one aspect of technique. Another important aspect is the imparting of force to a given unit of tar-

The classical Horse Riding stance (Lion's Roar)

get area. To do this efficiently, the combined style employs the Chinese principle of 'stored' gin (power). Gin is held so to speak, in the form of kinetic or 'potential' energy, in flexed joints. These can be any and all joints in the body, capable at that moment, of transferring force into the target. Traditionally, this force is further described as being either chi , breath, air , or even sinking power.

In pure mechanical terms, the kinetic energy is transferred into actual impact force by a series of 'collapsing' movements, each of which is a strike in itself, and also adds momentum to next blow. For example, a downward striking finger blow, to the brachial plexus (nerve bundle behind the collar bone that supplies sensory and motor function to the arm) delivered with a flexed wrist, which itself then converts into a palm edge (hypothenar eminence) strike to the clavicle (collar bone)which again converts into a forearm and elbow strike to the ribs. All are given extra impetus by a forward projecting 'stomping' movement from the stance, and an exhalation of

Character '8' or Ape stance (Lion's Roar)

Twisting stance
(Lion's Roar)

breath, which allows further mass and momentum to follow through into the target. The above is an example of a 'multiple strike', and yet it only describes action on one side of the body. An expert practitioner would make a simultaneous contact engagement on the opponent's other arm, and against his support plane, usually by compromising his stance.

Inch Punch - Shades of Bruce Lee

There is yet another feature of destruction, which has become well known in popular martial arts folk-lore, that of inch power. This relates to the generation of power from very close distance. The Chinese style of Wing-Chun has become almost synonymous with its use and it was one of the first techniques with which Bruce Lee made an 'impact' on American martial artists.(1) However, as we saw above, the Bamboo Forest Temple Mantis is also renowned amongst knowledgeable martial artists, for being expert at the close range generation of power, and its application to vital points.

As well as inch-distance hits, the Mantis actually employs techniques that strike, re-strike or penetrate the target, from actual contact i.e. from zero inch distance! These hits are not 'pushes', but generative explosions of force, that penetrate the surface of the target with follow through. Sometimes, they will be delivered with an 'accelerated' single knuckle (phoenix eye fist in Kung-Fu). This means that a 'tucked back' knuckle, usually the middle joint of the index finger, is powered forwards, to penetrate the target, immediately following a first impact with say for example, the middle joint of the middle, ring and little fingers (the ginger or panther fist in Kung-Fu). Delivered as a vertical fist strike to the sternum (breast bone) and coupled with the accelerated knuckle as a 'contact' strike, this can be devastating.

Another variant, again against the sternum, is the 'collapsing palm'. Starting as a relaxed past-hand that lightly contacts with the fingertips against the opponent's sternum, the blow lands with a vicious snapping action from the palm-heel (thenar eminence). Follow through is generated by exhalation and a stomping action through the stance. I know from personal and very practical experience the lethal potential of this strike. I once had occasion to use it against an assailant, and struck his sternum with such force that it pressed against his heart, causing a cardiac arrhythmia and then, cardiac arrest. He needed emergency resuscitation and thankfully he lived, somewhat the wiser for his experience!

Armour Piercing Shots

Matching strikes to body tissue may be described as the armour piercing shot! This is an important consideration in the application of destruction techniques. **In general, bony target areas should if possible be struck with single knuckle hits.** The pain from receiving such a strike is excruciating, shocking and downright demoralising, though it usually takes a few moments to be felt and then actually increases, rather than wears-off, over time.

Also, the potential for imparting fracture injuries to the target is increased. With muscle tissue, once again the single knuckle strike

*Shooting stance
(Lion's Roar)*

*Stretched Cat or Bird
stance, with side facing
'gun-sight' guard hand.
(Lion's Roar)*

*Back Bow stance
(Lion's Roar)*

Forward Bow stance, with side facing
Lama gun sight guard hand
(Lion's Roar)

should be favoured. Understandably, martial artists have the tendency to 'build-up' muscle mass, both for power, and for protective purposes. However, muscle as a protective layer of tissue is most

effective against so called 'flat fists' or palm strikes. Penetrative finger attacks can harm muscle, although a lot seems to depend on the density and conditioning of the tissue itself. Single knuckle hits are paradoxically more effective against dense muscle

Basic Mantis On Guard position.

Standing Crane stance (Lion's Roar)

mass, as the muscle goes into spasm. The stronger the muscle, the greater the spasm and thus the greater the pain. Anatomically, there is no additional layer of protective tissue for muscle, and so it follows that there is no anatomical defence for an attack on muscles them-

selves; in effect, an armour piercing shot.

The muscles can be any skeletal muscle group, on the torso or any of

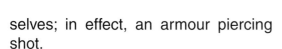

Alternative On Guard Mantis position.

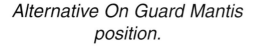

the limbs (including the head and neck). I have quite literally seen hook punches 'shot out of the air' by a phoenix eye hit on the twin head of the biceps muscle. One of my own students did this to me, (otherwise I would have hit him) and for my kindness, I was left with severe bruising on the impact site for nine months afterwards! (this was despite treatments with Chinese medicines).

Other soft-tissue areas on the body (fat!) can be struck effectively with any hand formation. Blood vessels are best gripped, or 'poked' with the fingers, whilst nerves should be struck in accordance with how 'superficial' or deep they are, relative to the surface of the body, and whether or not they pass over a bony surface.

Strikes with the hard edges of the exposed long bones of the limbs, can be very effective in inducing deep muscle spasm. Against the neck for example, a forearm blow even against a well developed neck musculature can cause occlusion (blockage) of the blood vessels underlying the muscles, leading to unconsciousness. In my experience, the effect can be virtually instantaneous, or follow a delay of a few seconds.

A further mechanism for unconsciousness arising from blows affecting the blood vessels supplying the brain is the baro-receptor reflex. Here, blood pressure is regulated locally in response to information received by the brain from specialised cells in the walls of the blood vessels. A sudden occlusion and re-opening of the blood vessels catches these cells out, so to speak, and they then send the wrong information to the brain, which in response lowers blood pressure, in turn leading to a transient unconsciousness; one long enough to finish off your opponent!

Attacks on joints or cartilaginous tissues such as the nose and ears can be enacted with a variety of natural weapons. As a general principle, strikes to joints are best delivered with knuckle fists (ginger or phoenix eye) or palm heels. Tendons can be struck too, particularly where they cross joint surfaces. A good example is the biceps tendon, which crosses the superficial aspect of the elbow joint. Muscle attachments are another good target. These can be at the ends of tendons as in the biceps example above, or alternatively at points of insertion into bone.

An unusual but very effective one to hit is the insertion of the lateral (side) compartment of the deltoid (shoulder muscle)into the humerus (upper arm bone).   This point is known anatomically as the deltoid tuberosity.   Attacks can be with single knuckles, but also with a 'rolling' or 'grinding' forearm action (like a saw).   This latter action is good against the triceps muscle, by applying force against the 'grain' of the muscle tissue, and in the opposite direction of its bony attachments. Incidentally, one reason that the biceps is such a nice muscle to attack is because it is not attached to the upper arm, and if struck, will pull violently against its attachments in the shoulder and forearm.

The eyes are a special example of 'soft tissue', consisting of muscle as well as blood vessels, a lens, and specialised light sensitive nerve cells. Some scientists actually consider the human eye not as a separate sensory organ, but rather as a forward projection of the brain itself. Naturally, such an important target is well protected; on an instinctive level through reflexes, and structurally through the orbits (bone around the eye socket) and the eye lids.

Attacks on the eyes feature in all martial arts systems. However, to successfully strike them is rather difficult, and can be a matter of luck as much as of skill.   Straight finger thrusts will of course severely damage the eye, if they make contact.   In practice this is unlikely, as the stiffened fingers can bounce or skim off target, and contact with the orbit bones can break even the most heavily conditioned fingers.

In the combined style, three general kinds of eye attacks are preferred: laceration, phoenix eye punching and contact thrusting.   Laceration here refers to the use of finger 'fan' techniques, that wipe across the eye at very high speed.   The fan can be delivered with a lead or rear hand, the latter being effective against 'square-on' centre-line fighters, who tend to believe on dogmatic grounds that your rear hand could neither reach them, or by-pass their guard. The leading fan is much faster than either a straight lead punch (jab or blast); backfist or even straight finger thrust.   It is a good alternative to either of the aforementioned, and has the ability to 'open' the face of an opponent.   I once saw someone not only instantly dropped by this strike, but also his face gashed from beneath the eye, right across the nose, and opposite cheek.

Phoenix-eye punching refers to a 'designer' eye punch, launched as a tight-hook, impacting with the bottom three knuckles against the orbit of the eye (lowest or little finger knuckle-against the temple) and the accelerated phoenix knuckle, penetrating the eye socket itself. Needless to say, this is a devastating hit, that can cause unconsciousness through sheering impact to the skull, as well as breaking the orbit bones and imparting a compression injury to the eye tissue.

Contact thrusting refers to the light contact of fingers or the thumb against the eye tissue, which at that moment then fully extend and thrust deep into the socket. This avoids the risk of damage to your fingers and assures accuracy and penetration. Many other variations for destruction against specific tissue types are employed. Grabbing and grappling in various guises are prime examples.

Grappling, of course, is a destruction method, satisfying both the balance breaking and the specialised tissue attacking criteria. In the combined style, grappling is employed using the same principle as the so-called 'stand-up' techniques. The body-clock and control planes work just as well on the ground as in any other dimension of combat. The choice of technique in any given instance is determined by the 'battle computer', which may naturally switch instantly into, and between, grappling or striking methods; freely and according to 'feel'. There is no limiting dogma such as 'grappling only' or 'blow before throw'. Computation, selection, and execution of techniques should be as natural as possible.

In my practical martial arts experience as a Liverpool Police Officer, grappling of one kind or another often featured as part of a street attack, or an arrest. Usually, if an attack is launched against a Police Officer, it comes from someone in a state of high adrenergic arousal, and sheer rage. Even today, most villains only 'go' for a Police Officer, once they've either lost control completely, or have cold bloodedly decided to 'put him/her away', as in an effort to escape arrest, or in an ambush attack. In such instances, I've found direct striking to be the more effective immediate response. However, where someone has had to be subdued, say in a situation where the Police were not the principal target, then grappling has often come into its own. I still remember the grappling 'advice' I got from some old experienced hands when I first joined the force: 'Grab em and hang on until he gets' tired'. Exactly what the 'em' was that you were supposed to grab and hang on to, was never specified, but... years later when a colleague and I were ambushed by a gang of a dozen youths, after fighting hard for our skins, I found myself understanding what was meant. In the court hearing that followed, the ring-leader of the gang pointed at me and said: 'That bastard grabbed me sack your honour!'

His honour reflected for a moment, and then pronounced the technique 'Most appropriate!!!'

Now, for attacks against heavily clothed or 'padded' assailants, broad contact areas should be favoured, such as palm heel, elbow, forearm; shin etc. Heavy padding tends to dissipate single knuckle hits, just like a bullet proof vest; the physics involved being very similar. The broad based contact area for strikes against padding actually helps impart 'pure force' quite effectively (just like a punch bag!).

Other related issues such as conditioning, and traditional protective exercises like chi-gung and so forth will be discussed later.

The apparently very sophisticated techniques and attacks outlined in this section are actually quite simple and efficient, provided that they are applied through an understanding of the system's guiding principles, and in particular contact engagement through the body clock, and the control planes.

In conclusion then, the system's principles work seamlessly together, to produce an overall clinically efficient result. The value in analysing them separately lies in the greater understanding that will come when they are blended back together once again. And remember: Grab 'em, and hang on till he gets tired!

The following section shows examples of techniques and gives the reader a break from looking at words...

(1) Bruce Lee developed what has subsequently been called the 'Power Punch' or '1 to 3 inch punch'. Lee demonstrated at Ed Parker's tournament in Long Beach, California in July 1964 and 'knocked them out' with his skills. Film actor James Cobern attested to the efficiiency of this short distance punch in a television interview on BBC2 with Mark Cousins, film critic, on March 11th, 2000. Lee sent him flying with it, and was prompted to take lessons from Lee on the basis of this experience. Other publicly acclaimed exponents of this art include James DeMile, (U.S.A.) and Jan Wright, (England) to name but two.

APPLICATIONS OF SOME LION'S ROAR TECHNIQUES

S1.1. Attacker skips in with mid section side kick.

S1.2. Defender steps back into twisting stance and blocks kick with elbow strike to the ankle bone

S1.3. Defender spins around with a whipping back-fist which is blocked by the attacker.

S1.4   Defender converts the back-fist to a grab and uses his continuous turning force to launch a toe-kick to the attackers groin.

S1.5. Working back of the attacker's body, the defender shuffles a cross kick to the knee joint to balance break.

S1.6. Finally, the defender finishes with a shuffle toe kick to the attackers throat.

S2.1. Attacker left, and defender right, in guard stances.

S2.2. Attacker steps forward with a straight blast punch. Defender steps to the outside and drops an overhead axe punch to the attackers biceps.

S2.3. As the attacker throws a second punch, the defender grabs the attacker's lead hand, steps in with a balance breaking stance manoeuvre, and executes a pivotal axe fist strike to the second punching arm.

S2.4. The defender finishes with a chicken's heart knuckle punch to the throat.

S3.1. Attacker left, and defender right, in guard stances.

S3.2. Attacker's punch is intercepted, by a right hook to the shoulder, and a left hand trap. Note the stance breaking step into the attackers support plane.

S3.3. The defender wrist locks the attacker's right hand, and axe hits his second punch.

S3.4. The axe hit converts into a downward palm strike to the jaw.

S3.5. Finally converting to a downward elbow ram to the sternum (and heart).

S4.1. Attacker left in guard stance, defender right in side facing Lama stance.

s4.2

S4.2. Attacker attempts a front kick to the apparently exposed groin of the defender, which is trapped by the defender's rear leg, (the arrow of the 'bow stance') moving up and through the midline to intercept the attacker's kick at the ankle.

S4.3. Seen from the opposite side, the defender utilises the kinetic energy in his bent ankle and knee joints to spin the attacker's kick 'off line'.

S4.4. Then the defender kicks to the inside of the attacker's thigh, to ensure his balance remains broken, whilst still maintaining contact with the line of the kicking leg.

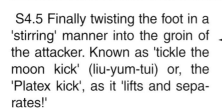

S4.5 Finally twisting the foot in a 'stirring' manner into the groin of the attacker. Known as 'tickle the moon kick' (liu-yum-tui) or, the 'Platex kick', as it 'lifts and separates!'

HOP GAR MANTIS KUNG FU • A SCIENCE OF COMBAT

S5.1

S5.4

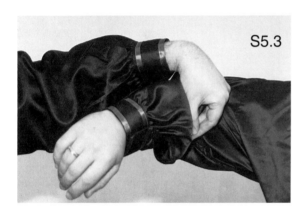

S5.3

S5.4

S5.1. Defender, left. Attacker right. Both in typical 'sticking hands position'.

S5.2. Defender hooks away the attacker's wing-hand block (bong-sau) by controlling the inner surface of the elbow joint. This principle is called 'follow the elbow' (huen jang).

S53.Defender strikes the biceps muscle on the defender's left bridge arm (tan sau) with a phoenix-eye claw (fung-an-jow). This has three striking points: the extended middle finger knuckle, and the gripping thumb and first finger.

S5.4. The defender finishes by converting the elbow hook to a 'down-and-away' grab, and the phoenix-eye claw to a squeeze point whipping hook to the point of the jaw. Note the simultaneous stance breaking technique.

S6.1. Attacker left, blocks defender right with a wing-hand block.

S6.2. Defender's rear hand grabs the wing-hand at the wrist, and applies a contact pressure hammer fist (gau-choi) above the elbow, to roll the attacker's arm down.

S6.3. Defender pulls the attackers arm across his body and applies breaking pressure above the elbow.Note how the defender has stepped inside the attackers centre of gravity.

S6.4. The defender pulls the attacker's arm further across his body rolling it into a wrist lock. The attacker's arm is also pinned at the shoulder and leverage applied against the elbow. The defender has slipped his arm under the attacker's, and delivered a mounted thumb Lama fist strike to the sternum. Note how the defender has positioned his lead leg further through the attacker's stance, to prepare for a sweep.

S6.5

S6.6

S6.6. As the attacker falls to the ground, the defender drops his full body weight against the attacker's shoulder joint, with his knee. Whilst simultaneously locking the arm, causing dislocation. The defender then finishes with a phoenix-eye claw grip to the carotid artery, causing unconsciousness.

S6.5. The defender simultaneously sweeps back and loops his arm around and strikes with the forearm on the back of the attacker's neck. As well as being a blow, this also applies equal and opposite pressure to the sweep, making it more effective.

S7.1

S7.2

S7.2. Defender then simultaneously pulls the attacker on to a palm strike and hook kicks with the toes to the groin.

S7.1. Attacker (right) launches a lunge punch. Defender engages to the outside with a hooking hand block.

S7.3. Following through, the defender breaks the attackers balance above the knee, and attempts a head pull to elbow strike, which the attacker blocks with his left palm.

S7.4. The defender shuffle steps around the attacker's stance and applies a finishing neck crank.

S8.1. Attacker (left), tries to 'tackle and take down' the defender (right), who is in a Lama guard stance.

←

S8.2. As the tackle comes in the defender relaxes back into a bow stance to 'receive' the incoming force. Simultaneously he slice blocks (fon-kiu) the attacker's right arm at the elbow, and delivers an elbow strike sideways to the attacker's temple.

→

S8.3. The defender (left) then moves forward into an 'ape' (or Chinese character for the number '8') Stance, locking the attacker's right arm with his left, and applying a headlock with his right arm.

S8.4. Stepping 180 degrees backwards into a bow stance the defender throws the attacker, with the attacker's whole body weight transferring through his neck joints.

S8.5. As a finisher, the attacker lands on his back, the defender pins his left arm by kneeling on the shoulder, applies phoenix eye knuckle pressure to this right shoulder, and slices his arm through the attacker's throat.

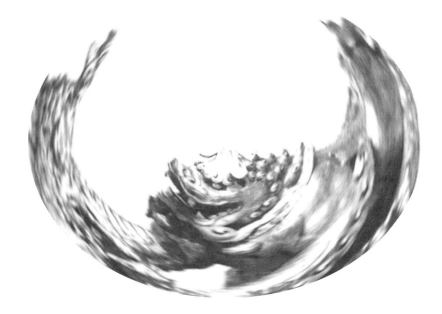

As we all know, pictures cannot replace movement. You need to try the applications out and see what happens; picking up the opportunities which you see any technique offers.

Tradition & the Combined Mantis

The combined Hop-Gar mantis system is authentic Chinese Kung-Fu and as such also features the 'traditional' martial aspects, to be found within any genuine Kung-Fu style. One of the creative tensions within the combined style is to effectively synthesise these with developments which should arise naturally out of the inter-relationship between East and West. **The purpose of this chapter, is to bring the eastern elements of the system into context,** but not without appropriate comment and contributions from the West.

Etiquette and Protocol

Etiquette and protocol should be considered. This raises the whole question of formality and informality. **This refers to the fundamentals of conduct and behaviour, to be found in any traditional martial arts school.** The Chinese are less obviously formal than say the Japanese, but don't let that mislead you! There is a strict hierarchical approach to training in traditional Kung-Fu. It's just that the **Chinese way of enforcing discipline and respect is more subtle. In the event, lack of proper respect means that you get taught nothing.** So, when it comes to sparring with your more dutiful classmates, you find yourself humiliated, by your own lack of ability and skill. Embarrassment usually means that students who undergo such an experience leave. Occasionally however, a more direct hint is required. In other circumstances, a student who turns out to be technically skilled but of 'bad' character may have to be 'dealt with' either by the school's master (Si-Fu) or, more usually, the senior students. Once again, the enforcing factor is humiliation (loss of face) which all Chinese understand culturally, as a degrading punishment.

In a Kung-Fu family acceptance into a traditional Kung-fu school means to be inducted into a new 'family'. The newest member is the youngest brother or sister. The oldest member is the eldest brother or sister. The teacher is called father (Si-Fu); his teacher is your grandfather (Si-Gung), your teacher's classmates are your uncles (Si-Bak for senior uncles and Si-Suk for junior uncles) and so on...
Ancestral reverence is a major feature of Chinese culture. Just like any Chinese family, the 'ancestors' are revered, which in this context

KUNG – FU : FAMILY RANKINGS

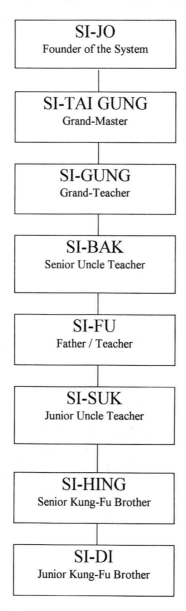

SI-JO
Founder of the System

SI-TAI GUNG
Grand-Master

SI-GUNG
Grand-Teacher

SI-BAK
Senior Uncle Teacher

SI-FU
Father / Teacher

SI-SUK
Junior Uncle Teacher

SI-HING
Senior Kung-Fu Brother

SI-DI
Junior Kung-Fu Brother

The basic family rankings and relationships in a traditional Kung-Fu School.

© **S.T.Richards 1999.**

The 'Cultural Genetics' of Martial Arts Forms

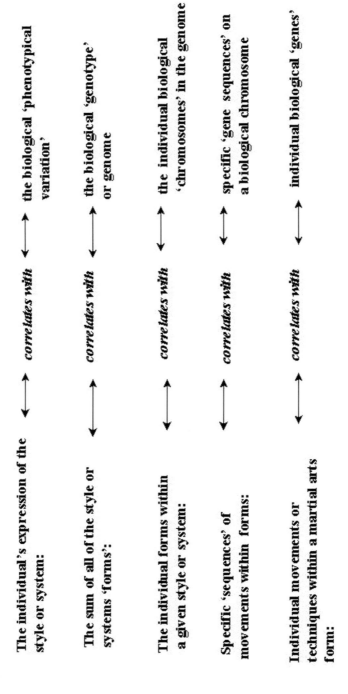

The individual's expression of the style or system:	*correlates with*	the biological 'phenotypical variation'
The sum of all of the style or systems 'forms':	*correlates with*	the biological 'genotype' or genome
The individual forms within a given style or system:	*correlates with*	the individual biological 'chromosomes' in the genome
Specific 'sequences' of movements within forms:	*correlates with*	specific 'gene sequences' on a biological chromosome
Individual movements or techniques within a martial arts form:	*correlates with*	individual biological 'genes'

Martial arts forms, are systems of 'cultural information'; analogous to the biological information, carried in the living bodies genes. The biological genes are not 'end-products' in themselves, and neither are the cultural genes to be found in the classical martial arts forms. If treated abstractly, then of course both are meaningless. However, understood intelligently, and contextually, both 'code' for an immense variety of situations and applications. The simple analogy between the information carried in biological genes and the cultural genes of martial arts forms allows the latter to be properly appreciated. © 1997 Steve Richards.

means your master's lineage. This is very important traditionally, as it is the authenticating factor, both for your teacher and for your own learning. All traditional schools have an 'altar' (Spri) on which is written the names of the past generations of masters, down to your teacher's teacher. The school's master opens practice in the training hall (Kwoon) by lighting incense sticks and bowing to the ancestors on the Spri.

Salutation between school members is also important. **Traditionally, there is no formal bow as in the Japanese arts, but the respectful use of the style's formal salute is expected.** The most common salute will be a variation on the familiar Shaolin left open hand and right closed fist, employed by all Chinese systems that claim descent from either the northern or southern Shaolin temples.

The Shaolin form of salutation actually appears to have been derived from the act of signaling membership of secret revolutionary clans (originally the Triads or Heaven, Earth and Man Societies), whose members swore to overthrow the Manchurian 'Ching' dynasty, in order to restore the ethnic Chinese (Han) 'Ming' dynasty. **The open palm means Ming, and the closed fist, Ching.** Sometimes, this is allegorised as 'the Sun (palm) shall overcome the Moon (fist)'. Nowadays, this salute has become almost universally adopted in Chinese martial arts, even by the Hakka (and therefore Taoist?) Jook-Lum Temple Mantis. The Tibetan Lion's Roar (Hop-Gar) with its Lama origins employs the joined vertical palm prayer posture of Buddhism, having no pretensions whatsoever to any link with Shaolin 'rebels'. It is actually possible to distinguish precisely between Shaolin derived systems, solely on the variation of the basic salutation that they employ. In the combined style, the Shaolin orthodoxy is employed, except when using Lama salutations at the beginning and end of Lion's Roar forms.

Loyalty to the extended kung-fu 'family' is understood as loyalty to the ancestors, the style and to its unique traditions. Like all 'kinship' bonds researched by anthropologists, this loyalty factor is somewhat elastic, in that depending upon a perceived threat, it can include, or not include, loyalty to related styles and families, religious sects, ethnic groupings or to the whole of Kung-Fu and the nation of China itself. Many traditional schools are informal about the question of uniforms, others have definite dress codes.   Generally however, kung-fu schools adopt a 'collective' image, that gives some degree of separate identity from other styles, or even branches of the same system.   There is less formality and indeed 'uniformality' than in the Japanese arts, for example but such codes as do exist are expected to be observed.

The more commercial developments of the Chinese martial arts tend to exploit uniform as part of their packaging, often displaying garishly bright and fancy patterned clothing.   Overall however, it is not possible to judge the quality or authenticity of a Kung-Fu school by the standard of the uniforms worn by its members.   Some of the best schools may 'dress down' by western standards, but then so may some of the worst. In the combined Hop-Gar Mantis style, plain western tracksuits and training shoes are generally worn for routine practice, and traditional uniforms, reserved for more special occasions, such as Chinese New Year, or public demonstrations.

In traditional circles, ranking is a function of three variables:

Are you a master or a student?
Are you a senior brother (Si-Hing) or a younger brother (Si-Dai)?
Are you an 'in-door' or a public student?

In theory at least, the status of 'master' is un-challengeable, provided it is conferred by your peers from within your system, and recognised by your peers from outside of your particular style.   The main factors are legitimised descent from an authenticated lineage and the development of character and ability.

Seniority

The rule of seniority for students in a traditional Kung-fu school follows the 'time served' principle, except where the master chooses one or more students to become his in-door or closed-door disciples. They may or may not have been Si-Hings prior to their selection. Outstanding loyalty, character and ability are the usual criteria, although occasionally nepotism takes a hand.   In practice however, **the passing on to a family member (usually a son) of the leadership of the**

style or 'family' is rarer than may be thought. Where it does occur, it is wiser to base it on merit, otherwise the style will degrade and perhaps even fracture into separate branches, thereby defeating the object of the authentic transmission of a tradition. These chosen students, known in Chinese as Yup-Mun Dai-Gee, are therefore to be groomed as successors to the master, in carrying the style into the next generation.

The in-door students get special, usually private, training, and learn the complete tradition. They pass through a secret ceremony known as the Bai-Si swearing loyalty to the master and the style's ancestors. Closed door students are not chosen lightly, and to be made one is the highest accolade a student can receive.

In Chinese tradition, there are no equivalents to the Japanese coloured belt and black belt dan gradings. There are advantages and disadvantages to this. The advantages lie mainly in the development of a 'core' of talented individuals, who can authentically translate a living tradition into a new generation. The disadvantages include the enormous 'wastage' in students that this approach creates, and the lack of a graded incentive to learning and achievement. It also means that students are unable to measure their progress against that of students from other systems by an objective 'bench mark standard.

Nowadays, the more strict professional protocols over gradings are beginning to break down. Coloured belts or sashes have been introduced by many schools, as have master grades, along the lines of the Japanese system. In the combined Hop-Gar Mantis style, modern grades including externally accredited 'Dan' grades are awarded, alongside the traditional 'family' ranking system. The 'In-Door' designation is still used to distinguish between ordinary students, and those preparing for master status. This way, the best of the old is synthesised with the best of the new, without compromise either to tradition, or to progressive thinking (please refer to the lineage charts at the end of this book, for a list of in-door students, who are externally accredited Dan grades, and authorised teachers of the system).

Stances

Rejection of the classical is a feature of modern times. Stance training is literally the 'foundation' of traditional Kung-fu. In recent years however, it has received a lot of criticism for being antiquated, irrelevant and without practical value. The same goes for classical footwork, which in effect is moving 'in stance'. The result has been either the rejection of traditional stances and footwork altogether, or more usually, their relegation to the practice of 'forms' (katas - see below). Even in the latter case, **inadequate attention to stance training means that the standard of forms practice is abysmal,** which is then seen as demonstrable proof of the uselessness of both; a kind of circular, negative reasoning. Some modern practitioners of the Chinese martial arts, who are influenced by these ideas, tend to use a rather poor imitation of western boxing footwork, as if as soon as they spar or fight, all that they have hitherto learned just evaporates like morning mist... so much for Kung-Fu!

Going back to the original premise, that classical stances and footwork are useless, is it in fact sound reasoning? Like with anything else, to answer this question meaningfully, we should address the fundamental issue of context. **Taken out of context, anything can seem inappropriate or just plain wrong.** What then is the proper context for classical stance and footwork training?

Stance and footwork training as are related to efficiency and therefore causality. The older methods of training, particularly in the public or 'out-of-the-door' classes, have provided some just reason for the rejection of apparently rooted and highly stylised stance and footwork practices. In essence however, **the traditional methods are very rational, provided that they are not treated as kinds of ends in themselves.** Rather, in the terminology of western logic, they should thought of as examples of efficient cause; that is, something that brings about, or makes other things, 'happen'.

Just as in classical dance, proper stances and footwork allow for the development of balanced footwork and coordination. This is even more important in the martial arts, wherein, not only must your own balance and weight distribution be addressed, but also that of your opponent; often working against your own. Classical stances do promote balance, and the footwork promotes the clean and efficient transition between postures, in response to changes, in combat. **Stances are both stable transitional platforms, from which to launch techniques, and also, 'ramming and jamming' methods, used as weapons, in themselves.**

In traditional Kung-Fu, the old maxim that the feet lead, and the hands follow still applies. This apparently contradicts some 'post-modern' approaches to the Chinese arts, which reverse the formula, and state that the hands move first, or that a blow should land before completion of a stance change, or step.   The latter viewpoint is fine, insofar as the object is to drop weight and momentum into the target, but, if the practitioner is unskilled, he is in great danger of over-reaching himself, through displacement of his centre of gravity.   The traditional approach fosters the development of balance, and quality technique. Indeed, **in the practice of classical forms, the quality of the footwork is the fundamental skill which determines the level of achievement and performance.**

The traditional 'horse' (stance) training in the Combined Style is used in an intelligent and informed way.   They are not used to 'test' students motivation, nor as the main method of building up strength and stamina in the lower limbs.   **Forms practice is used to teach the precise and proper use of footwork, in a structured way.**   The ability to move freely, appropriately and in balance is thus developed.   **I have found that the learning and execution of good traditional stance and footwork methods enhances students' learning, and gives an edge of balance and mobility over opponents in real fights.**

Each stance and posture is studied for its strengths and weaknesses, and students are encouraged to test their own 'designer' stance-breaking attacks, under the pressure of actual sparring against a determined opponent.   They are also encouraged to 'feel' how to move appropriately during contact with a partner's mass, momentum and energy, as these determine to a great extent the functionality of a given stance or footwork manoeuvre. Specific two-man exercises are taught, involving resistance training against the legs, and the use of single and double poles (staffs), to develop sensitivity, power and balance. In the combined style, the use of stances and footwork is not abstracted out from related factors such as kicking and grappling. All of these need to be taught, and practiced together, as a single integrated whole.

On balance (so to speak) the combined style prefers the traditional attitude towards stance and footwork training, although elements of the post-modern approach are included, as derived from the Lion's Roar system.

(Please refer to the sections on 'kicks', 'sensitivity' and 'practical practice', below.)

Classical Forms

Classical forms play a major role in traditional Kung-Fu. The practice of formal routines, handed down through the generations, is at the very heart of Chinese Kung-Fu. However, as with many other aspects of tradition, **the classical formal exercises are subject to much controversy, with many people now suggesting that they should be dropped from study altogether.** To traditionalists this is unacceptable. To lose the forms is to lose the style, simple as that. So, what are they really, and why are they practiced?

The forms are a kind of living library of techniques, that map out the history, development and spirit of the style. The Chinese are conservative about their forms, so adding to them or deleting movements from them, are very serious matters. Specific forms may have a history of many centuries, and even provide a link to the style's founder. In the forms are to be found all the essential building bricks for learning the style.

The post-modern critique of classical forms should be examined. **Critics, of the more dismissive persuasion, regard forms as highly stylised abstractions; meaningless for real fighting; and so altogether useless.** Such people tend to fall into the 'post-modernist' category of martial artist. Post modernism is a movement in art, philosophy and social science, that rejects all claims that anything can be explained or approached through a single method or school, of any kind. Its fol-

The limita-
tions of
classical
training
are real...

Bruce Lee's
approach was
in the
post-modern
vein...

lowers tend to be eclectic and claim that they take the best of everything, to create their own personal approach. Along with their rejection of forms, these people tend to underrate technique saying that they themselves prefer to keep things simple, thereby implying that others are complicated by too much technique, and are therefore impractical or even unreal. **The post-modernists also show a definite preference for fitness and athleticism, the overall effect being a cultural drift Westwards, and away from the East.**

As a justification for this, **post-modern martial artists with a Chinese background often point to the rationalisation of forms that has occurred in the Yip-Man branch of the Wing-Chun style, which now contains only three empty hand routines.** Some of Yip-Man's followers have stated that it was found to be impossible to reduce the style still further, say down to one form, which is why the three familiar ones have been retained. The post-modernists take this as justification for being able to further reduce th**eir art, by deleting all forms, so going one better than Wing-Chun. The Wing-Chun system is often considered as being grounded in empirical science, so, if you can out-do them by analysing forms out of existence altogether, then you must be even more scientific!**

However as we shall see in the philosophy, it isn't quite that simple, and a lot of problems arise when that viewpoint is taken. **Traditional criticisms of forms is not in any sense unknown.** Notwithstanding the rivalry and 'putting each other down' attitude that exist between different schools; the traditional critique of forms tends to be organised around the quality of technique, and the correctness of the form's actual content, and sequence of movements. Over time, variations in technique and sequence are bound to arise, and some of these are actually traceable to the influence of a particular teacher. **Generally, Chinese teachers, will above all else, look at the quality of the footwork in a form,** as this distinguishes advanced and accomplished practitioners from all the rest. This has a practical 'spin-off' value, in that good stance and footwork give support to hand and leg techniques. If you watch a Chinese Kung-Fu forms demonstration, always look at the footwork. Poor quality performers, rush through their forms, trying to move as fast as they can. This leads to incomplete or unfinished movements, loss of balance, and indistinguishable stance changes. Mediocre performers may be able to 'squat low' in a horse stance, thereby suggesting strength and power, but as soon as they have to move between stances it all goes wrong. The best performers understand the nature of their forms. Each form will have its own tempo and rhythm, which will probably vary from point to point, in the performance. The execution of power, stance changes, breathing and mental attitude will be just right. Small movements, or angles become very important.

Traditionalists do not regard the cultivation of these skills as irrelevant for practical use, far from it. **However, if forms are not learned properly, both individually, and overall as a concept, then they can be harmful.** So what's the position on forms in Hop-Gar Mantis Kung-Fu?

The Combined Style is derived from two traditional Chinese/Tibetan martial arts systems, and as such, it has carried over much of the traditional perspective on the positive value of forms training. The Lee-Yin-Sing branch of the Bamboo Forest Temple Mantis is actually a very rationalised system. In fact, there is only one form, in the whole of this style! Known as Sup-Sam-Jik or the 'Thirteen Roads' the entire teaching of Great Grandmaster Lee-Yin-Sing is summed up in this single routine.

Great Grandmaster Lee was a shrewd man, and a very hard practical fighter (as were, and are, his surviving students!). He formulated a way of preserving his style's principles (being founded upon these rather than anything else) by the creation of a single long form, comprising thirteen sections or 'roads'. All of his senior students were taught the fundamentals and principles of the style, and were then expected to constantly pressure test themselves in 'gong-sau' or hard-hand' real fights. The form was used as a kind of informal ranking system. The more of the form you knew, in the correct sequence of course, the higher your status.

From my research it seems that Great Grand-Master Lee would permit his students to teach, even if they knew only four sections of the

fist... formations...

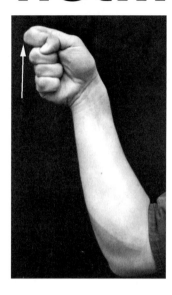

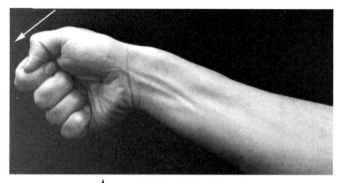

Classical
phoenix eye
fist form.

Alternative
classical
phoenix eye
fist form with
'mounted thumb'
safety position.
***
'Tucked back'
and mounted
phoenix eye
knuckle fist,
prior to
acceleration
into target.

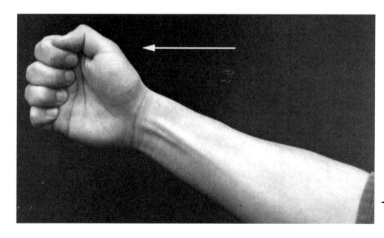

Mid-position of
accelerated
phoenix
eye fist strike.

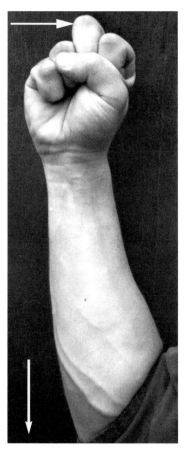

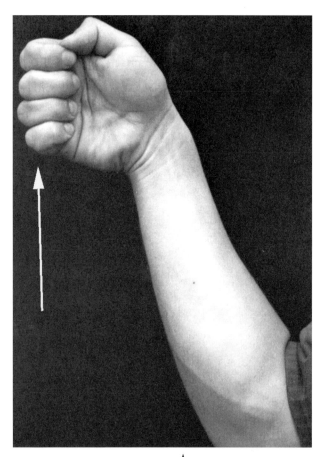

Chicken's Heart fist form showing 'proud' middle finger knuckle as striking surface.

Ginger fist form - striking surface is the 'serrated' edge of the fore-knuckles.

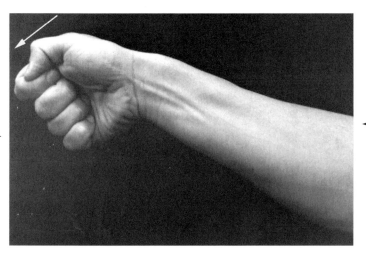

End position of accelerated phoenix eye fist at point of impact.

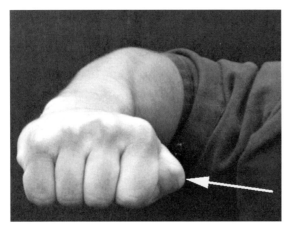

Lama fist form - front view - showing 'mounted' thumb position.

Palmar view of Lama fist form, showing 'mounted' thumb and fore knuckle squeeze point and 'scrapping' striking surfaces.

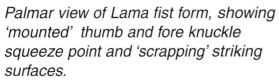

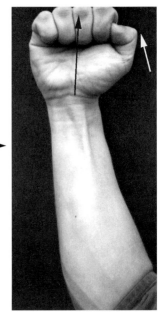

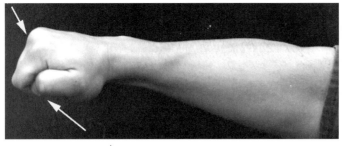

Lama fist side view showing 'mounted' thumb and main knuckle striking surfaces.

form, which is less than one third of its total length!

The main thing was what could be called 'back-engineering', which means the ability to derive the correct applications, from the principles of the style, or vice-versa. Here, we see an example of a very reduced approach to a classical system, with only a single form. This has led to an interesting position, wherein every Chinese master of the

'Mounted' thumb Lama hook punch into vulnerable neck areas.

Lee-Yin-Sing branch practices this form differently. The differences are sometimes slight, but at other times very marked. The main factor seems to be the personality and character of the teacher in question, as this is 'stamped', so to speak, on the form. All

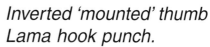

Inverted 'mounted' thumb Lama hook punch.

share an understanding of the principles, and so recognise the deeper connecting 'truth' between them, that is otherwise hidden by their superficial differences in practice.

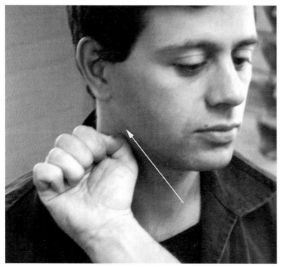

The Tibetan Lion's Roar family of systems is very different. In the Tibetan styles, there is now a very wide differentiation of forms. Some are shared between branches, others are unique either to one branch, or even a single teacher. Some claim as little as eight hand forms, others nearly a hundred. The original style had eight hand forms, just as it had eight stances, kicks, punches, speciality hands and so forth. However, what links all of these branches together, apart from a common physical origin, is the notion of guiding principles. Here then, there is shared ground with the Mantis system, and room for the development of a generative synthesis. Some practitioners of the Lee-Yin-

Sing system have close contacts with other branches of the Southern Mantis family, and also with other Hakka schools. Accordingly, some teach forms from these other sources, along with the original Lee-Yin-Sing form.

In synthesisng the combined Hop-Gar Mantis system, I took account of this, and introduced some southern Mantis sets from the other (UK) Jook-Lum Temple branch, as well as devising new sets, based on developments of the principles in the Lee-Yin-Sing form. I then did the same with the Hop-Gar, keeping some of the original forms, and adding or formulating others. These 'new' forms have been viewed and approved of by some of my Chinese teachers, as well as by the technical committee

'Mounted' thumb Lama hook punch into twin head of biceps muscle as a destruction technique against an attacker's punching arm.

of the British Council for Chinese Martial Arts (BCCMA): which is the U.K. Sports Council Governing Body for the Chinese martial arts.

There are eighteen hand and eighteen weapon forms in all, nine in each category, either derived or developed from traditional Hop-Gar and Jook-Lum Temple Mantis Kung-Fu. The exact number of forms was set not for any mystical or religious purpose, but as a reasonable number to allow progression, and understanding of the two complementary parent systems that go to make up the combined style; in particular, their practical guiding principles; those which define the very essence of the parent styles.   The forms retain their originating context and character, in that there is no combined 'form as such, and indeed this has proven to be the most workable approach.

Anthropology of Forms

The anthropology of forms, as a practical study, sheds more light on our subject.   The new and specialised study of martial arts anthropology was introduced as an academic discipline by me in a paper presented to the first international conference on martial arts held at the Sports and Exercise Science faculty of Manchester Metropolitan University, in July 1998. The paper was called, 'From post-modernism to dialectical syncretism: understanding the anthropology and cultural evolution of martial arts systems'. It was subsequently published and housed at the university.

This discipline is concerned with the study of the martial arts as a product of the evolutionary psychology of human culture.   The approach to the study of martial arts forms is to consider them as 'units of cultural inheritance' analogous to those units of biological inheritance: the genes.   Genes are of course, coded systems of information, that although simple in themselves produce the bewildering complexity of life on our planet.   The persistence of genes between generations of offspring is determined by the process of natural selection. Those that impart advantages in the struggle for survival, are more likely to be passed on to the next generation. Those that are not may fall by the wayside.

Martial arts forms are systems of cultural information which are passed on to future generations of martial arts students.   Like their biological correlates, they 'code' for functions and behaviours, that are far more complex than may be inferred from an analysis of their basic structure. Again, in a similar fashion to biological genes, martial arts forms must be read correctly for them to be of any use.   Biological genes have specialised molecules known as messenger ribonucleic acid

(MRNA) and transfer ribonucleic acid (TRNA) to correctly read and apply the function of any given gene. In the cultural genetics of martial arts forms, the interpretation and applied derivations of any given sequence of a form requires the conscious interpretation and therefore understanding of the whole potential for its application. Consciousness is here emphasised, because without this decisive factor, it is impossible to contextualise the apparently abstract information contained within a form. It is actually more efficient for forms to have this abstract quality, as the act of conscious interpretation allows a much greater amount of information to be carried in a relatively short sequence of movements (as in a digital computer). **In former times, lacking the advantages we enjoy today of video technology and even of printed books, martial artist teachers needed a system that preserved the fundamental information of their style, and allowed it to be passed on to future generations. Forms were the ideal information medium for the preservation and transmission of the style's cultural 'code'.**

Failure to correctly read the code of a form means that its information will at best be latent or at worst either misapplied or even lost altogether. This leads to at least three possible outcomes:

1. The particular movement in the form is passed on wrongly and remains so in the school.
2. The form is passed on without the particular movement.
3. The movement is passed on wrongly but someone, through study and application, re-interprets the wrong movement correctly, based on factors which lead to the correct interpretation. Factors such as principles and contexts and comparisons.

Critics of forms, who have not yet understood their true cultural and informational significance, would do well to look outside of the usual sources of martial arts wisdom, in other words to science and academic philosophy, in order to gain a more objective and informative perspective on their art. **It is irresponsible to reject forms out of ignorance.** Imagine a microbiologist rejecting DNA simply because it appeared to be just strings of meaningless molecules!!! The 'knee-jerk' post-modern negation of forms is similar; it is ignorant in the extreme and anti-cultural.

In conclusion then, the study and practice of martial arts forms is a vital aspect of a living tradition, which allows the inheritance of cultural information by future generations of martial arts students. The techniques in the forms are like genetic sequences, which although they are not end-products in themselves, nevertheless 'code' for an inestimable variety of applications and situations. **The reading of this code requires intelligence and diligent practice.** The post-modern rejection of forms can serve to remind us of the dangers of not reading their information content correct. The wholesale denial of their value is grossly one-sided simply because it emphasises only the negative.

The Hop-Gar Mantis system fully incorporates the intelligent use of forms into its syllabus, whilst maintaining contact with the decisive context of practical reality. The system's forms are derived either directly from the traditions of its parent styles, or newly formatted in the spirit of their guiding principles.

Specialised Hand Formations

Speciality hands are the signature 'tools' of the combined style. All styles of traditional Chinese Kung-Fu employ specialised hand and fist formations, which can be taken as signature tools for the system in question. In the combined Hop-Gar Mantis system, the following signature hand and fist formations are employed:

Phoenix eye fist or 'Fung-an-Choi', a single knuckle fist, employing the proximal (nearest) interphalangeal joint of the index finger as the striking surface. The first photograph (p.128) shows the basic form of this speciality hand, with the thumb placed posterior (behind) to the distal phalanx (end finger bone). The second photograph shows an alternative and perhaps safer form, with the thumb positioned on top of the interphalangeal joints. The third to fifth photographs show a sequence illustrating the 'accelerated' phoenix eye fist (unique to the combined style). Starting from a 'tucked-back position', the phoenix eye knuckle is accelerated through the mid position, and into its extended striking position, augmented by a sharp downwards motion of the wrist (note that this wrist action is not always required, but that it does increase end-point delivery of power).

The phoenix eye fist is found in both Jook-Lum Temple Mantis, and the Lion's Roar styles. It is used as a destruction technique, and the fist itself may be angled in any orientation or plane, relative to the target. The accelerated phoenix eye version of this strike was developed by me whilst researching improvements to the 'contact hitting' potentials of the Mantis style. I later incorporated it into the combined Hop-Gar Mantis system, and, I can attest to its real-life stopping power, from its practical use in street confrontations.

In strict traditional training, it is usual to 'condition' this fist (see below). However, in my experience it is only necessary to practice the correct form of the technique, and to support the fist through development of strength in the forearm and hand.

Anatomical targets for this fist form are typically vital point strikes against nerves, blood vessels, muscles, joints and soft-tissues (such as the eyes and the windpipe), as well as bones, including those of the hands, feet, shins, knees, hips, wrist, elbows, temples, sternum and collar bones.

Chicken's heart fist or 'Gai-Sum-Choi' is another single knuckle fist, this time employing the proximal interphalangeal joint of the middle finger. This fist form is also known in Chinese Kung-Fu as the 'Dragon's Head'. Less common in application than the phoenix eye, it is favoured as an 'add-on' for uppercuts', and vertical strikes to such targets as the biceps, the nose, the solar plexus and the sternum. Occasionally, it is 'hooked' into the attacker's arm, or used as a 'first impact' strike, to be followed-up by an accelerated phoenix eye 'contact hit', from the same hand. In tradition, this fist form is mainly featured in the Lions' Roar style, as the Mantis prefers the phoenix eye, and/or our next speciality hand... the 'Ginger Fist'.

Ginger fist or 'Gern-Chi-Choi' is a common fist form found in many martial arts, wherein it is usually referred to as a 'fore-knuckle' strike. However, what sets the combined style apart is its versatility in application of this fist. It can be delivered from just about any angle and in any plane, from within contact distance with the target. It is employed with

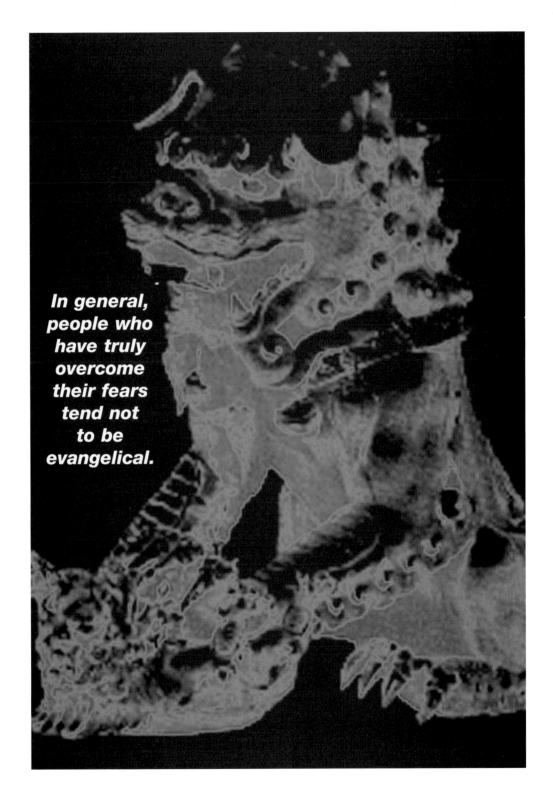

> *In general, people who have truly overcome their fears tend not to be evangelical.*

particular usefulness against long or flat, bony targets, joints, blood vessels and dense muscle masses such as can be found in and around the upper leg.

Within the combined style, there are various alternative names for this fist form, including charp-choi (stabbing-cut) and Si-Ji-Choi (lion punch). It also lends itself well for accelerated phoenix eye add-ons, and is a favoured strike to penetrate an opponent's guard, above the elbow joint, travelling from the outside in; either towards the mid-line, the floating ribs or the neck.

Lama fist or 'Lama Kuen' is basically a 'flat fist' form i.e. one without any forward protruding knuckle formations. What distinguishes it is the positioning of the thumb on top of the knuckles, instead of the more familiar covering of the middle phalanx bones, on both the first and middle fingers. Many practitioners, on first witnessing this hand form, seem disturbed by the apparent vulnerability of the thumb positioning, in particular the 'exposed' interphalangeal joint (knuckle).   Understandable as this concern may be, in fact the mounting of the thumb in order to stand the joint 'proud' is not only quite deliberate, but informed: the joint is used as a weapon!!

Hook punches are delivered with this fist formation, in a very tight arc, aimed at the opponent's neck, in order to strike not only at blood vessels, but also at the neck muscles themselves. The pain is excruciating (just try tapping yourself lightly on the neck or carotid with the mounted thumb joint; **at your own risk**). This can also be delivered as an inverted or pivoting strike, with the palm facing upwards.   An additional use is to slip an opponent's lead punch, and hook the mounted thumb joint into the twin heads of his biceps muscle; then accelerate a phoenix eye fist into the 'breath blocking point' (exposed ribs just below the lateral inferior or lower outside margin of the pectoralis major i.e. chest-muscle). Continuations from this point are at your discretion!

The other 'special' aspect of this fist form is that all the surfaces of the fist are for striking: The 'Chune-Choi' or penetrating cut uses the front of the Lama fist; the 'Pau Choi' or cannon punch uses back; the 'Cup-Choi' or raking punch uses the palm and fore-knuckles; and the 'Gau-Choi' or hammer fist uses the hypothenar eminence (edge of the palm).

Obviously, this fist form is Tibetan in origin, being the fundamental fist of the Lion's Roar system. It is used extensively to attack point-mapped vital points, or more crudely, to literally 'smash' an opponent's limbs; torso and head.

Other special hand formations are considered next. Beyond the four principle fists outlined above, the traditional Hop-Gar and Mantis styles employ the full range of hand and fist formations found in Chinese animal based systems. All are incorporated into the combined style, alongside the trained use of striking surfaces such as the elbows, knee, head, forearms, shins and feet and so on.

Kicking Techniques

With kicks or 'Leg manoeuvres', traditional Chinese Kung-Fu exponents are rarely seen carrying out the 'abstract' repetitive punching or kicking as is routinely found in Shotokan Karate or Tae-Kwon-Do. Whereas it can make sense to isolate certain classes of technique, in order to hone them to perfection, to Chinese thinking it can also de-contextualise them and create an 'attitude' built around the repetition of basics. Where this does occur, it is hardly conducive to the learning of advanced techniques, or skilled reactions.

For example **the use of kicks in authentic Kung-Fu is always in the context of the overall situation;** footwork, stance changes and hand combinations freely interact with kicking, according to requirements. Indeed, some Chinese masters refer to kicking as being but one part of the broader category of 'leg manoeuvres'. Teaching this way, rather than isolation drilling, encourages students to 'think', although not everyone can take to it. Situations then become 'problems' of coordination; the solution being the right stance, footwork, angling and the delivery of whichever technique(s) are most appropriate. Of course all of this does not mean that kicks either are not, nor cannot be, trained in isolation from other techniques; it's just a question of discrimination and emphasis. This of course can make all the difference.

The striking surfaces employed for 'kicking' in the combined style include all surfaces of the foot, the shin and the knee. If the term is

Dimensions of Combat graph

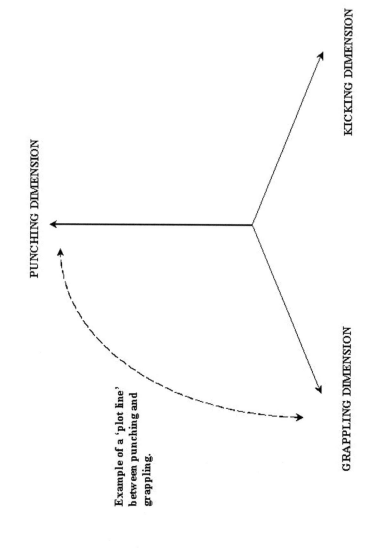

PUNCHING DIMENSION

KICKING DIMENSION

GRAPPLING DIMENSION

Example of a 'plot line' between punching and grappling.

A three dimensional graph with axis's showing the three fundamental dimensions of combat. Any given point can be plotted at a point relative to all others in any given dimension. This graph illustrates the fallacy of reducing 'range' which is a variable of distance, down to 'techniques', which are not ranges as such, in themselves © 1999 Steve Richards.

extended to include the broader category of leg manoeuvres then the thigh and hip should be counted, as in 'ramming and jamming' (stance work) as well as for levers and pivots for throwing; and barring and isolating for grappling. In Hop-Gar Mantis, footwear is always used, usually good quality training shoes. This allows a greater degree of realism, and also facilitates the use of destruction techniques both with the feet, and against them. Let's look now at some examples of kicks and their associated striking surfaces.

Dart kick or 'Biu-Tui' refers to frontal snapping kicks that utilise the toes for impact - hence the need for footwear! This is the lower limb equivalent to straight finger thrusts (Biu-Ji) although here the toes are curled down and tensed. Basic targets for this kick range from the medial and lateral malleoli (the bony protuberances either side of the ankle), through to the axilla (armpit) and the throat. More advanced developments involve 'hooking kicks', with the shoed toe points, against the inner thigh, the groin, the biceps, windpipe and carotid. Actual targeting depends upon opportunity and never upon dogma.

Tickle the moon or 'Liu-Yum-Tui' refers to a peculiar groin kick that lands firstly on the upper and inner thigh, with the kicking foot medially rotated and in plantar flexion (turned inwards and downwards). Upon contact, the foot laterally rotates and goes into dorsiflexion (turned outwards and upwards) in a 'stirring action' against the testicles. This kick is also known as the 'playtex kick': as it lifts and separates!

Springing kick or 'Tan-Tui' refers to any example of a springing-compression type of action, involving strikes with the foot. The most common variants are downwardly directed attacks against the knee, ankle or foot. Striking surfaces are either the heel or outer edge or sole of the foot. Obviously, as with all kicks, the orientation of the target relative to the kicker is important. Spring kicks against a prone opponent could easily include the head or neck region.

Flying kicks or 'Fae-Tui' refer to a whole range of jump kicking techniques, some of which resemble those found in more familiar martial art systems. In Hop-Gar Mantis, they include the use of 'stiff leg' kicks, either double or single, whilst airborne; jumping dart kicks (single or double); cyclone kicks (jumping crescents); butterfly kicks (360 degree flying back-crescents); jumping knee strikes (single or multiple). Also, the more specialised use of jumping kicks that utilise the 'dropping' of mass and momentum into the opponent, by arcing body weight into the air, but impacting just after a supporting leg makes contact with the ground. These kicks tend to be both faster and safer than those that attempt impact whilst still fully airborne. Striking surfaces include all those of the foot, the knee and in particular the shin.

In practice, jump kicks are mostly employed as part of a combination that may include elbows or 'dropping-weight' punches and stance breaking attacks.

Shuffle kicks refer to low-line kicks against the support plane of the opponent, involving shuffling kicks from alternate feet. They 'work-back' off the target to add momentum to each other, and can develop into low-to-mid-to-high level combinations, or back again.

Crescent kicks can be high, but tend to be used against a 'low orientated target' i.e. the head of an opponent whilst he is squatting or turned sideways. Thus high striking kicks can be delivered from a balanced position. It all depends on the relative height, movement and momentum involved. They can be executed either inside-out or outside-in. Impact is with the sole of the foot, but occasionally the ball or heel make isolated contact. A 'flicking' crescent kick (inside-to-out) is sometimes used, the action of the foot being similar to the playtex kick. Here the target is the chin or windpipe.

Sweeping kicks or 'Soh Tui' incorporates the traditional Kung-fu sweeping kicks, and scissors take-downs. Also deceptive pulling and diverting actions that penetrate the support plane, either of a moving or stationary opponent. Striking surfaces include the arch of the foot, the sole, heel and shin.

Intercepting kicks or 'Jeet Tui' include any kicking actions that arrest the opponent's momentum (forwards or backwards). The most common are kicks to the hips (points 5 and 7 on the torso clock) and 'sliding jams' against the lateral aspect of the ankle (leading aspect of the support plane). Others are 'cross kicks' against the lower limb or stance break-ing 'rams'. Leg 'traps' refer to any action involving contact engagement with the opponent's leg-bridge. The techniques can involve balance breaking, stomping, treading, sweeping, destruction and 'following the line' of the leg, from 'ground-to-groin'.

Another factor of importance in kicking is keeping the hips 'in-plane', which means parallel to the ground, and to each other as much as is possible. **Kicking techniques that involve displacement of the hips 'out-of-plane' are slower, less balanced, less direct and more prone to blocking or interception.** Essentially, your own head height should remain constant during kicking, or become lower due to the bending of your supporting leg. Overall, as kicks are generally used as part of an enmeshing pattern with the opponent's movements, they should not be telegraphic. Following the hips in-plane rule also adds to power. As an exercise, try positioning a heavy bag so that its base is at your own groin height. Then execute a fast snap kick to the bottom of the bag, lifting the hip of your kicking leg upwards and out of alignment with that of your supporting leg. Then try a second kick, this time keeping your hips par-allel. The second kick will be both faster and more balanced. Experiment with a partner by trying such kicks from a variety of dis-tances and angles. Concentrate on maintaining head height and align-ment of your hips. Also look at chambering opportunities that arise quite naturally from the various stances and footwork positions. This will help awareness and generate faster multi-level combinations.

Sensitivity Training

Sensitivity training is an important part of training. It includes sticking and pushing hands. Sticking hands (Wing Chun's chi-sau in Cantonese), along with the 'pushing hands' of Tai-Chi-Chuan, are the most familiar examples of sensitivity training to have arisen from the Chinese martial arts. However, this familiarity should not suggest a complete description of such phenomena. Other Chinese systems as well as many non-Chinese arts have similar forms of training. In the Mantis for example, a variety of drills involving contact between the prac-titioners' arms are routinely employed. They range from hard chie-sau or 'grinding arm' exercises, through to two and three man soft mor-kiu or 'feeling the bridge' techniques.

Feeling the bridge or mor-kiu exercises are quite different from other apparently similar methods of other styles. Rather than follow a repetitive cycle of interaction and a limited variation on contact breaking, mor-kiu simply involves either the sending and receiving of energy (force) in variable amounts, without any attempt to block or re-direct its flow. The purpose is to truly develop sensitivity, so that the passive partner in the basic exercise just receives incoming force and follows returning energy, as in the ebb and flow of the tide.

The active (sending) partner, varies speed, direction and force randomly, noting the ability of his passive partner to adjust accordingly. The sending and receiving is not limited only to the arms. As the basic exercise develops, so the leg bridges become involved and are co-ordinated dependently or even independently with the energy exchanges through the arms.

A more advanced development involves two senders and one receiver. One sender for each of the receiver's arms. In this variant of the exercise, a receiver may have to contend with different speed and power ratios through both his arms and legs at the same time. These ratios will interact and exchange in complex ways, fostering the development of advanced sensitivity skills. In the three man exercise, it is possible to further develop difficulty by changing the rules so that the receiver has to send through one bridge whilst receiving through the other, and then to be randomly instructed to switch between them.

Blindfolded mor-kiu exercises are employed, and provided that contact is maintained, this variant is actually easier (see principles chapter) than the sighted version. The blindfolded exercise is made more challenging by 'unseen' engagements and dis-engagements on both arm and leg bridges,and random changes of partner or partners. Still the object is the same, to develop sensitivity. Active aspects of combat such as interception and destruction are not included in this exercise. To do so would be to confuse the issue and may lead to the mistaking of the skilled exercise for something more real. In practice, the combined style has found it productive to keep the sensitivity and combat drills separate.

The body-clock and sensitivity can be usefully brought together. In the combined style, the mor-kiu exercise is overlain on to the body-clock and control planes so that an understanding of spatial positioning and energy for the whole target is developed. This then contextualises sensitivity by giving it an appropriate aim. Following this, targeting and destruction can follow quite naturally and efficiently, in a real situation.

Sensitivity training and real fighting is highly controversial in the martial arts at the present time. Wing-Chun is frequently criticised for mistaking the exercise for reality, and for hypothesisng a non-existent or 'manufactured' range. In my honest opinion the latter statement concerning a non-existent range has some validity, but only because there is a general misapplication of the term range anyway; so to criticise one misnomer with another merely adds to the error. (see principles chapter above).

Judging Range in Combat

The dimensions of combat brings into focus further important questions. The 'range critics' of Wing-Chun confuse a variable of distance (range) with a classification of techniques (trapping). Often these critics talk of punching, kicking and grappling ranges, whereas in reality these are more like dimensions of combat. **Just as space has three physical dimensions: length, breadth and depth, so combat has a number of dimensions that make up its potential totality.** The length (distance-range) of a given line in space is best seen in relation to the dimensions to other lines. It's the same in combat. The graph (see page 140) allows a conceptual point to be plotted for any potential action ranging from a 'pure' technique to any combination, in any given dimension.

All supposed ranges are 'relative' and only have any meaning at all in so far as they have context. Abstraction is a fool's game. In fact there is nothing 'un-real' about Wing-Chun's techniques. Indeed I would go so far as to say that any martial artist (particularly a non-Chinese stylist) would benefit from a proper study of Wing-Chun, as a bench-mark for their own ability to cope with and develop bridging skills. Some of Wing-Chun's critics would get a nasty shock if they tried to beat that system on its own ground. They might even find themselves being hit from a non-existent range!

It should go without saying that sensitivity and grappling go together. In the martial arts as a whole, the approach to the interaction of these subjects is markedly varied. In the combined style, there is the synthesis of the Mantis derived mor-kiu and sam gwan sensitivity principles, with those of the vertical and ground grappling techniques of the Lion's Roar, all of course overlain onto the body-clock and control planes.

As a basic exercise for grappling, following on from the mor-kiu sensitivity drills described above, the Mantis cum-na-kiu (Cantonese 'grab and seize the bridge') techniques are employed. In their most elementary form, these involve single handed grabbing, seizing, escaping and countering applications, against the opponent's arm bridge, concentrating on the sam gwan, in response to his attempts to grab and seize your own control points. The exercise is developed by employing both arms, and by adding the leg bridge dimension (such as chi-gerk, 'sticking leg'; chie-gerk, 'grinding leg' and chon-gerk, 'destroying the leg').

The 'horizontal' (ground) dimension, is merely the application of body clock/plane and destruction techniques. These include chokes, strangulations and neck cranks, as well as the usual vital point strikes. However, neither grappling dimension should be over emphasised through abstract practice. A further contextual consideration is the intermediate phase between the vertical and the horizontal, which involves acute awareness of relative spatial positioning and energy, and the ability to further switch the direction or focus of response. In Hop-Gar Mantis, grappling is opportunistic, arising naturally as and when the flow of combat requires. It is no more an end-in-itself, than any other classification of technique.

Conditioning

'Conditioning' in Chinese martial arts generally refers to specific rituals, exercises and drills for toughening both striking surfaces, and potential target areas on the body. Methods include respiratory training, the development of internal energy, hardening through striking against a partners limbs, the use of punch bags and wooden dummies, and the application of traditional herbal medicines and massage.

All authentic traditional systems include these practices, and they have a long history of proven effectiveness. However, they must be applied with caution. **Lessons learned from scientific western medicine suggest that it is unwise to attempt heavy conditioning of bony surfaces through repeated striking of hard objects.** Serious malformations of bone can arise, as can infections or even diseases such as arthritis or osteocarcinoma (bone cancer) brought about by trauma to bone and joint tissue.

The application of traditional medicines is not necessarily safe either. There have been cases of serious adverse reactions, and the contents of some herbal medicines have been shown to be carcinogenic (cancer causing agents). **Respiratory training too must be undertaken with caution.** People who suffer for example from asthma, hypertension (or other cardio-respiratory disorder), epilepsy, phobias, mental illness and other ills, need to take particular care when undergoing such practices (see below). Generally, chi-gung exercises designed to improve resistance to pain or tissue damage from blows involve moderate to high degrees of hyperventilation (here defined as breathing in excess of the body's physiological needs). The same phenomena can be seen in Okinawan Karate's Sanchin Kata. The resistance to blows involves muscular tension and analgesia, induced by hyperventilative changes in the body's acid-base (pH) balance. Effectively, this is a 'trance state" and any gains are not carried forward outside of being in that altered state of consciousness (once again see below).

In the combined style, traditional methods of conditioning are studied, but so also are western scientific methods, based on sports and exercise science and appropriate medical pathology. This way, the best of the East can be synthesised with the best of the West, to the benefit culturally and scientifically of the student.

Again, like conditioning above, internal energy training (chi) is included in all authentic traditional Chinese martial arts systems. Such practices are not restricted to China, or even the East in general, and are in fact found the world over, having been practiced for millennia. From an anthropological perspective, the obvious questions centre around the different explanations given by cultures for apparently the same phenomena. In the West, what passes for chi in the East is referred to as 'healing energy' and is routinely generated by natural healers from a variety of schools. It is also known to hypnotherapists as 'magnetic energy' as identified by the father of hypnosis Franz Anton Mesmer (from which the term Mesmerism is derived).

For the scientifically inclined martial artist, it is interesting to see if the development of so-called internal 'chi' energy does in fact require the cultural context of traditional martial arts training, or can the same effect be gained by another method? With respect to healing, although the 'energy' alleged to be involved cannot yet be measured scientifically, controlled double blind testing on burns patients has been carried out in the United States, which gave statistically significant results showing a marked effect on the rate of healing and a reduction in scar formation. Clearly, this suggests something real is happening. The self-reports of people who have experienced chi-energy and western healing/Mesmeric magnetic energy, indicate that they are in fact the same phenomenon. However, what is clear is that for the western practitioners there is no necessity for lengthy training or special breathing practices. Indeed, this author, as a practitioner of scientific holistic-medicine and hypnotherapy, has been able to produce chi-gung effects, including its 'projection at a distance', in a matter of only a few minutes, in trainees with no previous experience, and without laborious and secretive training in breathing or 'spiritual' practices.

The hare or the tortoise? Simply put, there is a difference in desired learning rate between the modern West and the traditional East, that may be likened metaphorically to the fable of the hare and the tortoise. The message being 'slow and steady wins the race'. Perhaps, but it also depends on the context of the 'race'. If a student wishes to be absorbed in the eastern cultural process, then he should expect a slow and steady progression, under the guidance of a qualified master (if he can find one!). If, however, the student wishes to gain a trans-cultural perspective on a deep, linking phenomena, that could otherwise be 'disguised' by the differences between specific cultures, then he may wish to take a quicker route, and one that is located in his own (western) tradition.

It is often said that patience is a virtue, and that the Chinese style of teaching, and rate of traditional learning, ensures that only the most highly motivated and deserving students learn the highest skills, and deepest secrets.   In an ideal world, this would be true.   However, much also depends on the integrity of the 'master', which is so often taken for granted, and sadly not always deservedly so.   The traditional 'apprenticeship' approach can also dis-include 'quality' students, and may also serve to maintain the status of the master.

In the Combined Style, students are freely introduced to the variety of possible routes to learning and to the competing explanations for the phenomenon of internal energy. In truth, **as the Greeks knew well, you cannot give knowledge away to those who just aren't up to it.** Nature is aristocratic, yet given a fair chance, the best will emerge, even from the most unpromising of beginnings.   A basic faith in the ultimate self-regulation of human nature is all that is needed.   The rest follows naturally.

Please see the chapters below on Philosophy and Mental Training, and Kung-Fu for the Street, for a further discussion on this very important area.

Attitudes to Breathing

As we saw above, **specific respiratory training regimens are involved in many aspects of Chinese martial arts, and these are potentially dangerous.** The health benefits of 'correct' breathing are rightly emphasised, but this presupposes that the correct method is both known and practiced.   As in all things context is decisive.

Changes in breathing are a common feature in the induction of trance (hypnotic) states.   Physiologically, breathing directly affects the brain through changes in the acid-base (pH) balance of the body.   In solution in the body fluids which include blood, interstitial (between cells) fluid, and cerebrospinal fluid, carbon dioxide (CO_2) exists as carbonic acid. Now, contrary to what most people are still taught at school, CO_2 is not just a waste gas, indeed it has several vital functions, including the regulation of signals at nerve junctions in the brain. Breathing regimens that promote hyperventilation (see under chi-gung above), involve loss of CO_2 (acid) which leaves the body in a more alkaline state. The immediate effect is a change in the acid-alkaline balance of the brain, which is conducive to entering trance like states, and can even produce hallucinations or symptoms of psychotic illness.

As outlined above, hyperventilation need not be the obvious 'panting' and rapid breathing most of us would recognise, and in scientific respiratory psycho-physiology, to qualify as a hyperventilator, a subject need only slightly increase the rate, or reduce their depth, of breathing.

Such subjects become more 'suggestible' and easily influenced, both by others, and by their own ideas, which may themselves be misleading or otherwise distorted. Trance like states and respiratory induced alkalosis can increase pain threshold (witness the 'testing' in a performance of Karate's Sanchin Kata), but they also facilitate 'state dependent learning'. This means that the learning or other gains made in that state are not carried forward beyond the 'trance' but are locked within it. The exception being the persistence of susceptibility to suggestion.

Other potentially dangerous factors include the predisposition for smooth muscle tissue, as typically found in arteries, and in the lungs, to go into spasm during a respiratory induced period of alkalosis. This can result in a stroke, brought about by the increase in blood pressure, as the bore of the arterial walls supplying the brain narrows; a dangerous asthma attack; or even a fatal heart attack through coronary arterial spasm. Other possible consequences include epileptic seizures, even in people with no previous history of such illnesses.

Very careful consideration is taken over the teaching of breathing techniques in the combined Hop-Gar Mantis system. The possible negative consequences are simply too serious to be overlooked on the grounds that the methods are 'traditional'. I have published scientific research in the discipline of clinical respiratory psycho-physiology, and

Steve Richards with senior student Bill Wilson. The Unicorn is on the left, resting on the drum, and the Lion on the right. Ching-Wu Athletic Association 1987.

*"An
unexamined life
is not
worth living,"
said Socrates.*

presented a paper entitled, 'Hyperventilation, trance states and suggestion in the martial arts', at an international conference on martial arts, at Manchester Metropolitan University, in July 1998. This forms the basis of the approach to respiratory training in the combined style.

Mystiques

Many westerners are drawn to the oriental martial arts because of its supposed 'spiritual' dimension. From an anthropological and psychological perspective, this can be seen as a result of the dwindling presence of an effective living religion in modern western culture. Also, there is the well known 'compensation factor' arising from a too one sided physical development, which necessitates a compensatory growth of the 'spirit' for the sake of balance and harmony.

From the oriental perspective, however, things are often very different from the image presented in pop martial arts films and television. Whereas there is no doubt about the fundamental involvement of Buddhism (Chinese and Tibetan) and of Taoism, in the development of Chinese Kung-Fu, **the actual integral practice of these religious disciplines is not included in most styles.**

What is evident, if you are allowed to penetrate deeply enough, is the use of so-called spiritual practices that involve 'possession states' and the ritualised incarnation of spirits, known as: Sun-Gung and Sun-Dar (in Cantonese) to attack an opponent. At a deep-structure level, anthropologists see little difference between these practices and various 'occult' methods developed in the west.

Some westerners do take part in these practices, having been quite fully absorbed into eastern culture. The safety or otherwise of this is dependent upon context; it will be safe for some, but positively dangerous for others.In Hop-Gar Mantis, students are taught about the cultural significance of Sun-Gung and Sun-Dar, but are also introduced to alternative explanations for what may be going on, derived from psychology and anthropology. Beyond this, 'spiritual' training in its broader sense, and the martial arts, do have some complementarity, but it should be remembered that it is no more necessary to be a martial artist in order to be

S.A.B.R.E.S.

The Knowledge Necessary For Healthy Function

S for SLEEP.

Awareness of the quality and quantity required for peak performance. The basic natural function for the restoration of homeostatic competence and repair.

A for AROUSAL.

The ability to manage struggle, hassle, and frustration without excessive involvement of the sympathetic nervous system and adrenal medulla, (S.A.M. Arousal System). The ability to accommodate loss, defeat, and despair without over-prolonged activity of the pituitary adrenal cortex (P.A.C. Arousal System). The "general drive state" of the organism.

B for BREATHING.

Awareness and control, avoidance of the inappropriate and disordered patterns of respiration defined as hyperventilation. Disordered breathing leads to pH shifts towards alkalosis that act systematically on the orchestration of the bodies homeostasis. Breathing retraining must take account of respiratory centre resetting and possible shifts into acidosis.

R for REST.

The ability to be still and at ease without guilt feelings or displacement activity.

E for EFFORT.

The ability to make and sustain effort without excessive fatigue or exhaustion. Not exceeding 60 – 70 % of maximum effort thereby allowing a functional reserve for emergencies and a learned pattern of appropriate energy expenditure. Training in the Human Function Curve (H.F.C.).

S for SELF-ESTEEM.

The feeling of worth, confidence and control achieved by the employment of S.A.B.R.E. with the restoration of homeostatic competence and healthy psycho-social functioning.

Adapted From Dr Peter Nixon MD FRCP (with permission)
Retired Senior Consultant Cardiologist
Charing Cross Hospital and Medical School: 1999.

'spiritual' than it is necessary to be spiritual in order to be a martial artist.

'Dim-Mak' the delayed death or 'time of day' striking art is related to pressure, and vital point hitting, and ties in closely with traditional medicine (see below), Sun-Dar, and internal energy training. All traditional Kung-Fu styles include this aspect, and at first it may seem quite remote from western science. However, when the issue of vulnerability to strikes at certain times of day is considered, then there is some considerable supportive scientific evidence.

Chrono-biology is relevant here. In the West, there is the developing science of chrono-biology, or the science of 'body-time'. Essentially, this studies the regulation of biological processes over time. It seems that humans have cycles (or periods) of harmonised psychological and biological activity that last from ninety to one hundred and twenty minutes. **This is the so called ultradian rhythm.** Every twenty-four hours, the system as a whole goes through a major cycle, known as the circadian rhythm. Between ultradians, there are characteristic 'rest phases' that can last from ten to twenty minutes. During these times, humans are more vulnerable to injury, infection and illness, and also to psychological suggestion.

Clear pathways in the body have been identified as being involved in these regulatory cycles. Their governing systems are known as the psycho-neuro-endocrine system (or mind-brain-hormone system) and the psycho-neuro-immunological system (or mind-brain-immune system). It's obvious that a 'natural' observation, made in a traditional cultural setting, could, over time, quite easily deduce whether, and when, people are going through ultradian phase shifts and become vulnerable both to real physical strikes, and to the amplifying effects of considerable psychological suggestion.

Belief can kill, let no one doubt this. Many of the hundreds of reported cases of Black Magic or Voodoo induced deaths have on analysis been understood to have been caused by suggestion. People can destroy themselves, if their belief is strong enough. Incorporate this kind of suggestion into a martial arts system, reinforced either by strong or preferably slight blows, then the human mind and body work in concert to self-destruct. **Couch this in a system of fighting that also includes very real and workable pressure point strikes against anatomically weak targets, and you have a very powerful cumulative effect.**

In Hop-Gar Mantis, students are taught about the traditional cultural context for Dim-Mak, but are also educated in western scientific explanations. Advanced students are trained in hypnosis and suggestion, and are thus able to understand the underlying mechanisms, and to face their own vulnerabilities to negative influence and maledictive suggestion.

As above under 'Chi', please see the chapters on Philosophy and Mental training, and Kung-Fu for the Street, for a further discussion on this important topic.

Traditional Medicine

Once again, this is included in all authentic Chinese Kung-Fu, and forms part of a larger cultural or ethnic medical tradition, that has helped to sustain the world's most populous nation for historical time-periods! This said, the clear implication is that it is functional, and may even have some superiority over western scientific medicine.

In truth, the introduction of modern scientific medicine has saved countless lives that otherwise would have tragically ended. Nevertheless, the efficiency of ethnic Chinese medicine cannot be overlooked. It is particularly effective in orthopaedics (bone setting) and has much to offer in terms of herbal medicines and of course acupuncture. There is also a strong tradition of 'complementary medicine' in the West, and much of this dovetails with Chinese medical theory, at a deep level. Overall, Chinese medical practices are couched in the same cultural beliefs as their religions and their martial arts. Traditionally, Kung-Fu masters had to be doctors as well, in order to treat the inevitable injuries sustained during training.

My Lion's Roar teacher, Si-Fu Kenneth Liu, qualified in acupuncture and traditional Chinese medicine in mainland China, however, he is also a western trained and qualified pharmacist, and fully appreciates the need to link both together, into a more efficient whole. Combined Hop-Gar Mantis students are given the benefit of access to traditional Chinese medicine, but are also reminded of the strengths of western scientific medicine. The potential for the misuse of acupuncture theory by misappropriation to such things as 'meridian striking' and claims of scientific status for its theories will be discussed later.

Weapons Training

Weapons training is an integral part of Kung-Fu practice, and their range and diversity is quite bewildering. However, it is often said by post-modern critics that **training with traditional weapons has no practical value, and that along with learning classical forms, their practice should be discouraged or even eliminated altogether.**

If weapons are properly taught and practiced, then this opinion is not sustainable. The use of weapons enhances empty hand skills, both in terms of strength and fitness, as well as in cognitive 'software' developments, such as targeting, computation and anticipation. Such skills increase the potential self-defence capability of practitioners, and provide a sense of 'realism' concerning supposed defences against armed attacks. If you are truly familiar with a weapon, then you are much more likely to be able to judge what can or cannot be done realistically to defend against it.

Traditionally, weapons are taught after basic empty hand and footwork skills have been mastered. It is also a feature of traditional Kung-Fu that the master will often 'select' a weapon for special or exclusive development, by a favoured disciple. This can mean that some weapons are 'lost' to a particular generation of students, and perhaps even from a lineage, altogether. This is particularly well exampled in the Choy-Lay-Fut system of Chinese Kung-Fu. This style is famous for its vast range of weapon forms. However, only the most senior masters in the direct lineage of the founder, Chan Hung, know all of its weapon sets.

The weapons forms incorporated into the combined style arise directly from the parent systems, but like the hand forms, include some new

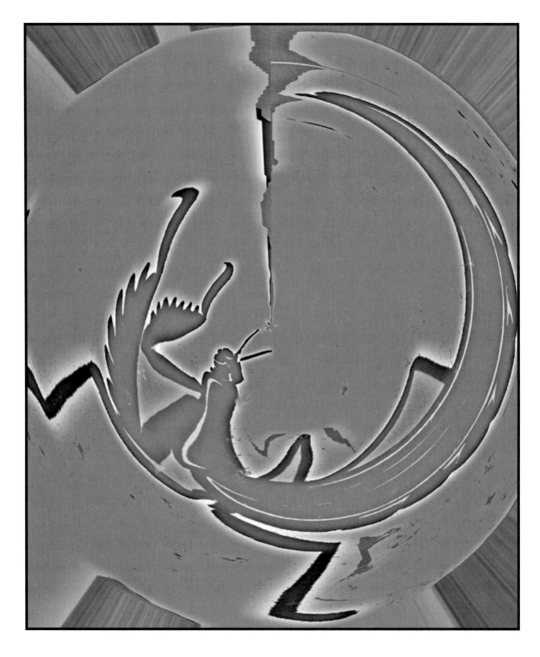

Praying Mantis systems developed in different directions, depending on several factors such as physical build, previous martial arts experience, and even religious influences.

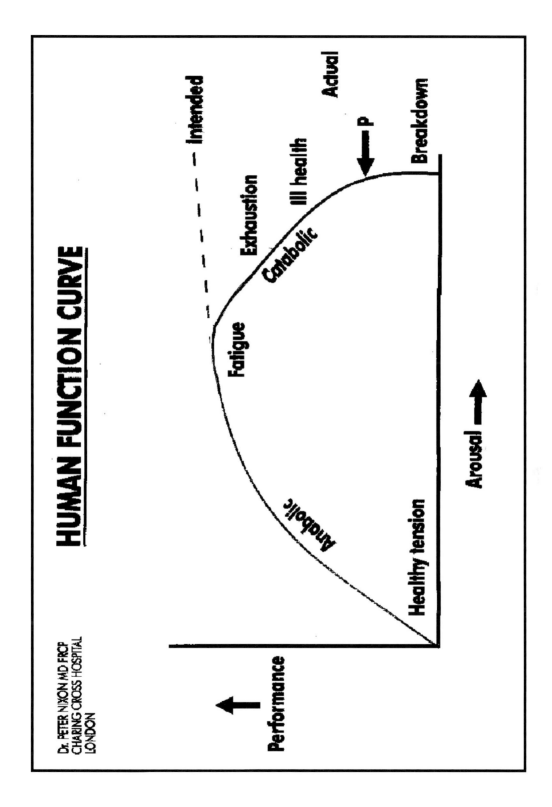

developments, unique to this style.

The Lama tradition employs the full range of traditional Chinese weapons found in both northern and southern Shaolin Kung-Fu. The Mantis is different. Weapons are usually taught in short two-man routines (forms) that are the basis for deriving all practical applications with that particular weapon. Hence, Mantis weapon sets, along with their empty handed equivalents, appear un-fussy and rather simple. The key, of course, is the ability to 'read the code' (see above) by back-engineering applications from principles.

The combined style retains a total of eighteen weapon sets: nine each derived from the parent systems. They are taught right from the beginning of a student's training, starting with the Mantis 'Eyebrow-Level-Pole', the Mantis Spear and 'Iron-Ruler' (Chinese Sai), both as two man sets.

Lion Dancing

In tradition, only Kung-Fu students may perform the Lion Dance. Just as in weapons training above, there has been no shortage of criticism in recent years of the supposed value of such training. It is a vital part of Chinese martial tradition, and no traditional school would be complete without such learning. Great strength, stamina and whole-body flexibility is developed through the Lion dance, which of course feeds back into beneficial gains in routine martial arts training. In the combined style, the southern Lion and the 'Hakka' tribes, 'Unicorn' dances are taught. This combines the traditions of the two parent systems, acknowledging their ethnic diversity. A fact appreciated by the Chinese as a mark of respect.

In conclusion, Chinese martial arts are an ethnic and cultural tradition, which cannot be wholly abstracted from their broader cultural context, without losing their essence. However, they cannot take root in western culture, without also adopting some western attitudes, and approaches to training. This process is dynamic and interactive, and will not progress uniformly: there will co-exist conservatism and post-modernity at the extremes, and a faster moving constructive syncretism (e.g.

combined systems), at the centre. **The combined Hop-Gar Mantis style, synthesises the best of Chinese tradition with the most efficient of western methods: both theoretical and practical.** It is a truly cosmopolitan system, and one that the Hellenistic Greeks would have understood well.

'Sei-Lo-Fun-Dar'
(Four Way Separate Attack)
Basic Tibetan Lion's Roar Form
and Applications

F1. Bodhisatva worshipping the Buddha (Lama salute posture).

F2. Opening the 'horse' with double 'fon kiu' or separating bridge hands, aimed at the inside elbow joints of an opponent.

F2a. Side view showing the 'staggered' position of opened horse stance, left leg 'proud'.

F3. Twist through to right side facing bow stance with a transitional 'long receiving bridge'.

F4. Complete the movement with a side facing gun sight Lama guard posture

F5. Step back with the left leg into a 'shooting stance' with cocked left fist, used to block downwards with the elbow.

F6. Spin 180 degrees into a left bow stance, with a simultaneous up-swinging cannon punch (pow choi). to block or strike).

F7. Step into stretched cat stance with right fore-knuckle punch (ginger fist). Stance is used to intercept opponent's leg; also kick preparation.

F8. Step back into a shooting stance with cocked downward elbow block (to cover incoming low attacks).

F9. Spin into front facing 'ape stance' (also known as figure of 8) .

F10.Launch a horizontal 'bin choi' or whipping backfist, so that it circles around the back of your body.

F11. Immediately fire upward swinging cannon punch with left hand following through at 360 degrees (complete circle). Angle of delivery towards midline of body; following inwardly pointing angle of knee. Twist waist for power, but keep stance rooted by bracing toes.

The previous move is repeated nine times with alternate arms in a windmill fashion, finishing on your left hand.

Complete as F9. But with the left fist cocked.

F12. Step back as a three quarters turn to the rear, with your left leg into a twisting stance (lau-mah).

F13. Drop down for 'iron broom' sweeping kick. Note the left fist is chambered for a 'swinging backfist'; right hand for hook punch. These must follow through simultaneously with the sweep.

F14. Completion of the sweep. Note the right hook punch and trapping rear (left) hand

F15. From sweep position rise straight upwards with swinging backfist (whip punch) into forward bow stance. The stance acts as balance breaker, following low-line engagement of the opponent's leg with the sweep, at ankle (support plane).

F16. Finish the action with a thrusting fingers strike (biu ji choi).

Note: F12 to F16 are to be performed as one continuous action.

Repeat F12 to F16 two more times, starting with the three quarter turn twisting stance.

F17. After completing the third sweep, step across to your right at 180 degrees, raise both fists upwards above your head for protection.

F18. As a continuous movement finish in a twisting stance with a double downward backfist strike.
Exhale on completion of the movement, brace your stance, and snap the wrists downwards.

F19. Turn leftwards through the twisting stance, into a transitional 'cat' with chambered phoenix-eye fist (fung-an-choi).

F21.Keep hips parallel, weight down onto right foot, simultaneously turn 180 degrees into transitional cat, with chambered downwards backfist (deng-choi or nail punch).Photo shows view from opposite side, for clarity.

F20. Drive through into stretched cat stance with phoenix-eye single knuckle strike.Turn 90 degrees left; repeat F20 punch; pull yourself around by moving lead leg, still balancing on toes. Repeat twice making four punches in four directions.

F22. Shows impact position of nail punch, and the forward weight balanced by the stretched cat stance.

F23. Step forward and through into the opposite stretched cat, delivering a full momentum overhead axe punch (pec-choi) diagonally through the centre line towards your left, and the opponent's right.

F24. Continue a 360 degree arc with the same fist form, and in the same stance, cutting down and through to your right and through the opponents left.

F25. Finish with ginger fist strike.

F26. Turn as in F21, but utilise hooking hand block.

F27. Step through as in F23, but with a hook punch (tsou choi) and trapping rear hand.

F28. In the same stance, pivotally chop with an axe fist to your right, to impact an attacker's punch at the shoulder or elbow joints.

F29. Same stance, convert axe punch into a round-to-straight 'chicken's heart' (gai-sum-choi) single knuckle punch. This turns inside arc of opponent's punch and impacts as a straight line hit, usually to the sternum or throat.

F30. Turn three quarters backwards through a shooting stance with a cocked left fist. Spin through with a left horizontal backfist and right hook punch.

F31. Complete the turn into a side facing bow stance and a left 'penetrating punch' (chune-choi). This is a straight punch launch off the hip, with a simultaneous spinning backfist strike to the rear.

F32. Step forward with the right leg into a parallel ape stance and deliver a left horizontal whipping backfist.

F33. Launch nine 360 degree cannon punches as in F11, same waist rotation, braced stance & angle of delivery. Finish on right.

F34. Twist into a leftwards bow stance at 45 degrees to the last ape stance and deliver a right phoenix-eye punch aimed at the solar plexus.

F35. Repeat opposite side. Note the chambering of the fists, and that F34 and F35 should follow as one smooth action, working back off each other.

F36.Step slightly forwards and across your midline into a right bow stance, left hand blocks downwards, and the right hand forms a chambered axe fist.

F37. Chop (axe punch) inwards, to the kidney region of opponent, with a simultaneous twist of the stance and waist. Draw left hand upwards towards the shoulder forming a chambered axe fist.

F38. Twist back against yourself drawing axe fist into open hand upper position; left hand back to lower position - twist away a grab made by your opponent on your axe punch.

F39. Step forward again as in F36, and axe punch as in F37.

F40. Turn right leg/foot 90 degrees to right, and draw both feet together, with left hand below palm up, and right hand above palm down.

F41. Lunge forwards with both palms turning over into their opposite plane. This is the 'soft dragon' (yau-lung). The lower hand checks, guides or traps, whilst the upper hand intercepts or strikes. Then repeat F40 to the opposite side

F42. Repeat the yau-lung to the left.

F43. Step through your midline into a forward bow stance, grab downwards, with a simultaneous leopard's paw strike to the eyes (pau-jow).

F44. Twist on your bow stance and use both arms to catch and upwardly deflect an opponents bridge.

F45. Twist into side facing left bow stance, left hand holding opponent's bridge arm as right hand first hits with heel of palm against pubic bone, then flicks fingers into groin. Squeeze and pull: 'monkey steals the peaches' (how-che-tow-doh).

F46. Pull back into a short or 'retracted cat' and chamber for an inverted (palm up) foreknuckle strike to the throat.

F47. Move forward into a stretched cat with the inverted strike to the throat.

F48. Drop your weight forwards onto your right leg and turn your rear foot into a shooting stance with chambered left fist, then, twist 180 degrees with a spinning backfist into a bow stance. Repeat F40 to F47 then F48, turning into F49.

F49 Having turned from the shooting stance in F48, you are now in a 'transitional horse', with left chambered dropping elbow block.

F50. Twist into a left side facing bow stance with a simultaneous left whipping backfist and straight punch (chune choi).

F51. Completion of chune choi.

Repeat chune choi with the left.

Repeat again with the right.

F50. Bring Form to a close with Lama Salute.

Issues of Health

Being 'let-down' by your body through a compromise in health is a great fear of many athletes. Such highly tuned minds and bodies can be easily defeated by the common cold virus. Indeed, it seems that the greater the fitness the greater the negative effect. 'Macho' martial artists might not like to admit it (perhaps for superstitious reasons) but they are just as vulnerable. The same goes for the effects of fatigue, or even a simple headache. All will reduce efficiency, whether technically or just plain physically.

This aspect of the 'fear factor' is usually repressed from consciousness, or if it is admitted then denied through attempts at positive thinking. Such thinking can be helpful, particularly at enhancing immune system responses to infections, through visualisation methods. However, it should be remembered that many of the symptoms of infection including high temperature or fever, are caused by the activity of the immune system. Therefore, if you use visualisation not wisely, but too well, then you may only increase your symptoms rather than remove them. Therefore, you should be prepared to utilise visualisation, in concert with proper rest and good nutrition, in order to reduce the duration of the infection. **Nobody gets away with breaking natural laws,** offenders are always caught and punished.

A very useful system for regulating physiological competence, in relation to the turbulence of the modern environment, has been developed by Dr Peter Nixon MD FRCP. Dr Nixon was involved in cardiac rehabilitation and the treatment of exhaustion at Charing Cross hospital and Medical School, London U.K. He was a mentor of mine during my occupational therapy training at that hospital, and later during my early years as a psychotherapist and psycho-physiologist in primary health care settings.

The effects of ill-health, fatigue and the natural, cyclical regulation of the body's systems, certainly affected my performance as a Police Officer, and on occasion caused near disaster for me in street confrontations. It is only because of my awareness of such factors, that I was able to reduce their effects, but even then many influences were outside of my

Hop-Gar Mantis Kung-Fu: the science of combat
Steve Richards figure © 1993.

Dialectical Syncretism

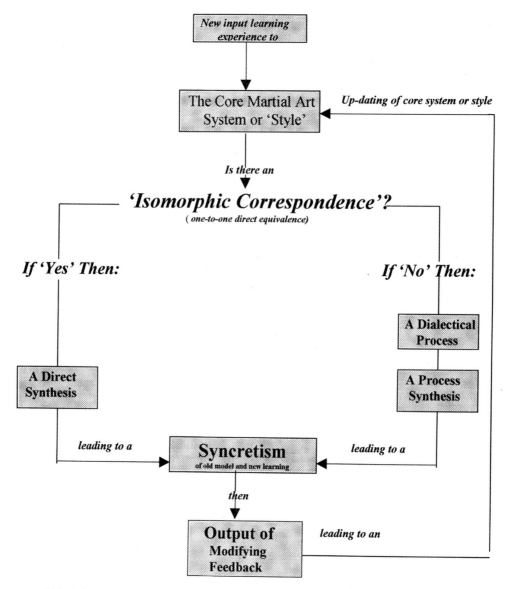

Dialectical Syncretism: modelling the on-going process of rational growth and development through the incorporation of 'new learning' into a core-martial arts system, thus facilitating the continuous evolution of an individuals personal 'style'.

direct control. It is of course like that for everyone, not just for the Police. However, in a law enforcement situation, working through rapidly rotating shifts; and having to face just about any and every human emergency suddenly and without warning; brings out clearly the underlying dynamics of both health and ill-health.

Issues of psychological health go hand in hand with physical health. Mind and body are like the opposite sides of the same coin; you never do get one without the other, and what effects one also effects the other. Many of the psychological factors involved in health have been outlined above under 'suggestion' as have the very real and disturbing issues of psychopathy and personality disorders in martial arts instructors.

Fear is the key, and today there is a fashionable martial arts industry arranged around the concept of fear. Some proponents of this approach claim to have 'conquered fear' and to be able to offer a 'real' approach to street combat, itself based in part on controlling or overcoming the psychological and physiological effects of this emotion. This is a very laudable intention and goal. However, it is a very big claim to state that fear has been conquered, particularly when additional claims are made about 'having no ego', and similar statements; (see above for the possible psychological dangers of this). People, including martial arts students, who may live in a state fear of whatever kind, are extremely open to suggestion, and therefore vulnerable to any ideology that claims to have solved it.

In general , people who have truly overcome their fears tend not to be evangelical. With evangelism, there should always be the suspicion that instructors have not in fact overcome their fear at all. On the contrary, they may be locked into a state of repetition compulsion, forced to continuously expose themselves to feared situations, in an attempt to convince themselves that they are 'O.K.' All of this masks deep inner uncertainties. The acceptance of limitations, and the re-framing of misinterpretations, are the stuff of real progress in the conquest of fear.

The idea of limitations is unpopular with some martial artists, particularly those who are one-sided in their physical development, and/or have little or no philosophical or spiritual education. An 'unlimited" personality will inflate like the frog in Aesop's fable, until it bursts. **It is not a weakness to integrate personal limitation, but a strength.** This is particularly important in teachers of the arts, as they have the responsibility to prepare future generations for their personal development.

Yes, incorporate training that is realistic and practical regarding the fear factor, but beware subliminal effects from people who may not be as self-assured as they seem. Human relationships are a 'field phenomenon' within which psychological infections take root through emotionally charged feelings of identity and suggestion. As a rule, look at what a martial artist does best. There you will find the key to their fear. The man who relies on speed is not likely to be afraid of a stronger opponent, but of a faster one! The technician, of a better technician, and the brawler of a stronger more aggressive one.

Every light casts a shadow; the brighter the light the darker the shadow. People naturally develop what seems most comfortable, but seldom have an answer for a better version of themselves. This is true for beliefs as well as techniques in the arts. In psychotherapy it is well known that people are most vulnerable to the weaknesses identified by their own world view. For example, Christians are vulnerable to suggestions of guilt or to the concept of Satan, as these are 'built-in'. It's the same with martial arts ideologies. If you want to know your true weaknesses, look into your own shadow.

Over-emphasis on physical training is always a danger. Many martial artists reach a point in their training career where they become almost fanatical about being 'fit' and train themselves with an obsessive intensity. This can be due to a number of variables. Firstly, being fit is a good thing, and worth striving for, and to maintain. Secondly however, exercise can be addictive due either to the release of natural opiate like substances, which provide a 'high' which in turn then requires a frequent 'fix'. Thirdly, many practitioners become disillusioned with their perception of the technical side of the arts, and in compensation over-emphasise fitness or muscular strength.

This latter point, the over-emphasis of the physical due to limitations or disillusionment with the technical, is in fact very common. It can certainly seem a very rational response to the observation that 'most styles don't work in the street' and perhaps the only response to the idea that 'no style works in the street'. The lack of real logic in these lines of reasoning has been discussed above, but sadly lack of logic is no guarantee that a given idea will not be influential.

Some styles or systems confer very definite advantages technically and practically over others. If an individual has had no true contact or learning of these systems, then he may well conclude (by sweeping generalisation) that all 'styles' are the same. This dynamic is at work in many cross-trainers and post-modern eclectics. It is equal and opposite to the ignorance of the 'traditionalists' whom they criticise for maintaining that their one system is the best. It is unusual for the eclectics to see this reflection of themselves, for who takes enough trouble to see into the darkness cast by their own shadow? As an issue of health, this emphasis on the physical may be reinforced by a narrowed consciousness of the technical in the arts, and an addictive 'high' on endogenous opioids, which at its worst results in a form of 'aerobic masturbation'.

The Greeks understood well the ideal of a healthy mind in a healthy body. This notion is accepted today as a natural truth, but the discipline necessary to attain it is often lacking. Learning how to reason, how to eat well and how to rest, were every bit as important as athleticism in the ancient Greek education for life. Contemporary martial artists espouse these virtues; let us truly live them!

> **Most students know the structure but few know the essence.**

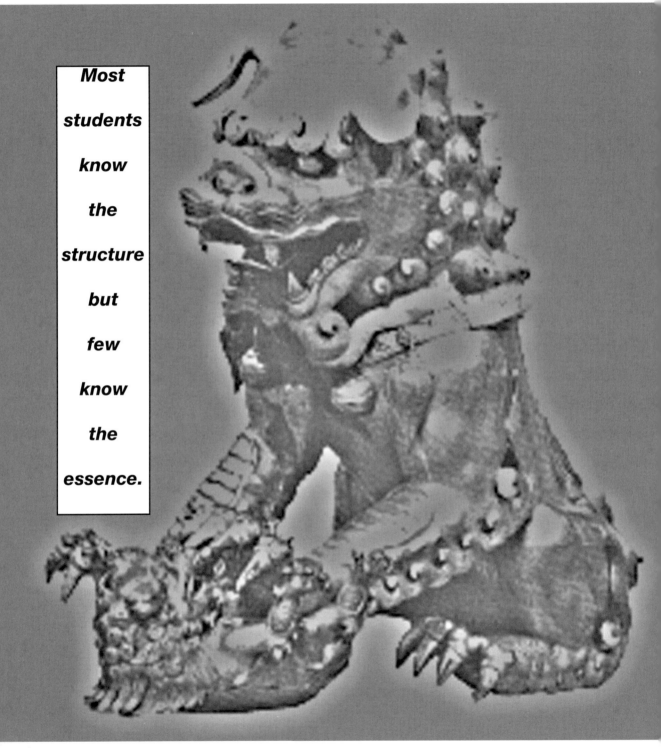

Kung Fu for the Street

This chapter deals with the controversial issue of the practicality or oth-erwise of traditional martial arts in street encounters. **It has become fashionable of late to berate classical training as impractical in the 'real' world,** and to advocate an approach based on eclecticism; cross-training, and preemptive striking. Each of these factors has merit, as well as a downside, and as with everything else, the decisive element is context without which nothing at all has any meaning.

Limitations of Classical Training

Once, **to even talk of limitations to the classical martial arts was an excommunication offence.** Now, howeve, the pendulum has swung the opposite way and the 'politically correct' attitude is to regard them as largely irrelevant or useless. Informed and educated martial artists are 'required' to be cross-training eclectics, with practical skills honed in real street fights. We saw above that there was nothing new in this current eclectic (post-modern) trend, and that it has periodically arisen as a gen-erative cultural dynamic, acting as a catalyst for progressive change. What is different today, is the media power in the representation and communication of these ideas. In the past, all creative change in mar-tial arts systems arose by breaking down older fixed systems. Our infor-mation technology age is simply speeding up the process.

Classical Martial Systems

Kung-Fu for example, entered this post-modern era, communicated via the informational and representational systems of the past. Many mas-ters of past generations were illiterate, and of course lacked video tech-nology for the preservation of their styles. **The classical methods of recording and transmitting the various styles to future generations suited the times, and the ethnic cultures of origin.** It's quite possi-ble for example to teach classical Kung-Fu to two distinct groups of stu-dents and get two entirely different results. One group will understand, and the other won't. Perhaps unsurprisingly this has been the norm, as Chinese culture is selective and discriminating in how it passes on its best knowledge.

Naturally, this leads to a situation where **most students know the structure but few the essence.** In other words a deliberate policy of 'wastage'. A spin-off from this is that the withheld knowledge takes on mystical suggestive power, which in the context of Chinese culture is encouraged, as it enhances status.

A negative aspect of this is that a good deal of Kung-Fu students can't use what they have learned, particularly if they have stuck only to the basic information taught in their system. Of course, this is true for all other oriental systems, that utilise the same traditional approach. **Sometimes, the best and most creative students, are not from the chosen few, but rather from the misled rest.** These exceptional people manage to apply their own intelligence and creativity to deciphering the 'code' of the style. They may go on to be outstanding masters of their original system, or perhaps to create their own new way.

In a post-modern context, these individuals would likely become cross-trainers or eclectics, abandoning with distaste, the ways of the past which had let them down so badly. Given that the martial arts have survived for so-long, and that in a Darwinian world (survival of the fittest) they could not have done so if they were truly unreal or impractical, how should contemporary students apply their learning for the street? **Well firstly, you need a good teacher, and secondly you need to be a good student.** Neither should be taken for granted, as the one without the other leads to nothing productive. Good teachers thoroughly understand their style and can translate it effortlessly into street encounters. Good students study hard as well as 'train hard', as success in Kung-Fu is as much a mental as a physical phenomenon. Good teachers hold nothing back and are willing to grow and develop in their relationship to their students, drawing out Socratically, the potential within their followers. Good teachers should also be exemplars in their behaviour, and should certainly not be violent psychopaths disguised or legitimised as ethical martial artists. **In the 'real world' however, such standards and such relationships are rare.** No wonder then that the traditional martial arts have largely lost their way.

In my opinion then, it is the responsibility of the teachers to teach properly to good students. This may mean that the uptake for training is reduced, as not everyone can take to the demands of personal tuition, (either teachers or students), but in the long-run it is probably the best way to preserve the best of the past. **Traditional martial arts do work otherwise they would never have survived.** However, today that survival is in doubt due to antiquated teaching styles, and the massive overproduction of mediocre students, who often through no fault of their own have been taught wrongly. Enter the cross-trainer!

Cross-training

The contemporary phenomenon of cross-training is a legitimate and intelligent response to the limitations of traditional training and teachings. However, as with all forms of eclecticism it has some severe weaknesses. Firstly, to be successful you need to have a good background in martial arts. In other words some experience of structure. **Learning that is not based on structure becomes aimless.** Secondly, if at all possible, gain your own experience. Eclecticism 'by proxy' or vicarious eclecticism is second-hand knowledge masquerading as the real thing. In that sense it is worse than the worst of traditional training. Students in this category are usually highly suggestible, relying on that facet of their nature to get them through life, being incapable of the self-creation required of truly efficient cross-trainers. The disappointment felt by these individuals at being floored easily by traditionally trained martial artists is painfully sad. **There is currently a cross-training industry flourishing, some aspects of which are very good, but others disastrously misleading.** Those that do mislead may well be fronted by popular personalities, who utilise suggestion techniques to manipulate people, particularly by reference to their unconscious fears. After-all, nothing conditions quite like fear, or pain.

Being 'Streetwise' - the First Essential

One of the main practical drawbacks of the classical approach to martial arts, is that it does not prepare students for dealing with instinctive responses to a threat, nor help them to train their general awareness. Both of these are so fundamental that they may be considered issues of personal survival. A new trend in the arts is to organise 'self-protection' training around basic principles calculated to give the optimum chance of street survival to anyone, regardless of background or training.

In my opinion, every new student who enters training at a martial arts school, should start with this approach first, and then only if they wish to learn a complete system, should they continue on. After-all, many people enter the arts to learn self-defence (or self-protection) and instead find themselves misled into something abstract and apparently meaningless. Peter Consterdine is an exemplar of this practical approach to street self-protection, and unlike many others, has impeccable credentials as a classically trained martial artist. His book 'Streetwise: the complete manual of personal security and self-defence' is without doubt the leading work in that field, and I would recommend it highly.

Learning Through Instinct

The most efficient way to learn something, is to make it as close as possible to an instinctive pattern of response. That way, there is no need to develop or even to rely upon finely developed skills. In 'pop psychology' the brain is often represented as divided into two halves: left-brain and right brain. The so-called left brain is said to house verbal; mathematical; rational and analytical skills. The so-called right brain: intuition; pattern recognition; music and feeling.

In reality the picture is much more complicated. These distinctions refer only to the left and right cerebral hemispheres, and do not in any way describe separate brains, nor do they both add up to the whole brain either. There are deeper, 'sub-cortical structures', that themselves contain all the necessary brain functions for the maintenance of life, as well as areas involved in instinctive reactions such as territoriality; aggression and sexuality.

Like other martial arts, Praying Mantis was influenced by the concept of Ying and Yang.

Basic pressure point attack: accelerated phoenix eye hit against the nerves and tendons of the wrist.

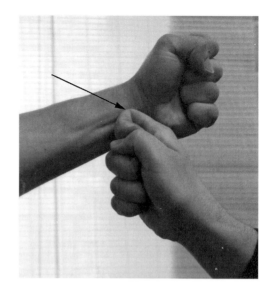

Ginger fist strike against inner surface of the wrist, by 'slipping' a lead jab.

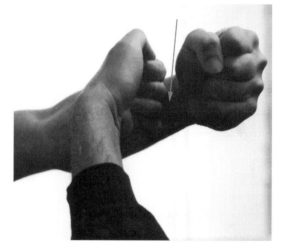

An accelerated phoenix eye strike to the carpal bones and nerves of the back of the hand after drawing out a lead punch.

A phoenix eye fist strike against an uppercut, impact on the twin heads of the biceps muscle.

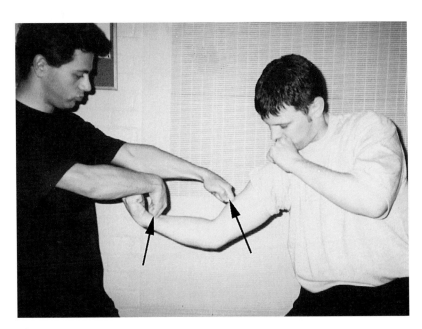

Double Ginger fist strike, impact on the biceps and wrist of a 'long' uppercut.

Accelerated phoenix eye strike to the 'breath blocking' point on the lateral aspect of the chest wall, with a simultaneous parry at the attacker's wrist.

Ginger fist strike to the acromion process of the shoulder joint (joint between the shoulder blade and the collar bone).

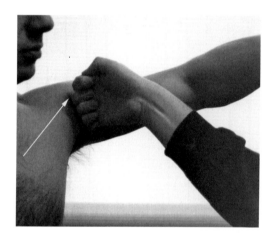

Accelerated phoenix eye fist, impact between the anterior margin of the jaw, and the right ear. The strike is 'bounced off' the attacker's right lead punch, as a parry, before converting into the hit.

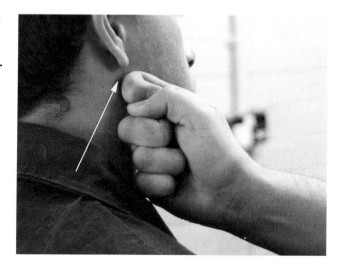

1. Hand position for palmar power slap (Lion's Roar) with the pad of muscle tissue at base of thumb. This striking surface is very hard, allowing for speed as well as impact in a pre-emptive strike.
2. Palmar power slap as a pre-emptive strike just as a left hook is launched.
3. Showing 'knock-out' potential of power slap; rear hand ready to deflect or parry.

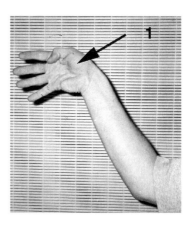

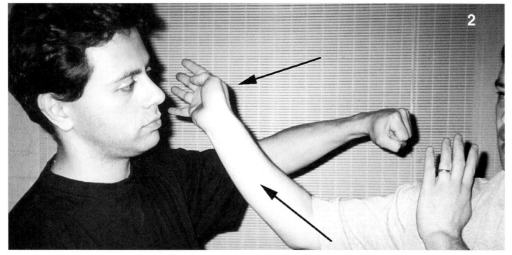

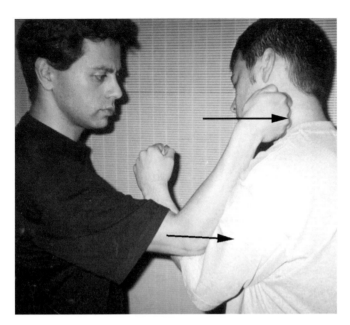

As a pre-emptive strike against an attacker taking a boxer's guard. Defender (l) uses a Ginger fist over attacker's left lead into the neck, whilst forearm and elbow slam into his arm, immobilising his shoulder and elbow joints.

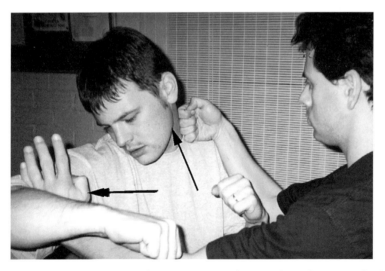

Same as above from opposite side shows defender's left hand immobilises attacker's right hook attempt by checking the elbow joint.

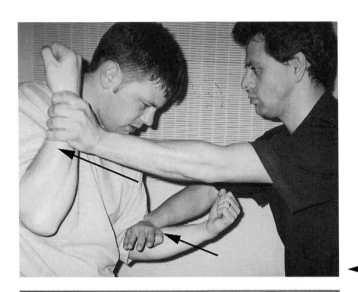

Attacker (l) tries a left uppercut from a boxing guard. Defender slice blocks the blow at the elbow joint, simultaneously grabbing and pushing attacker's right hand to immoblise it.

Attacker pivots his left from the blocked position into a high hook aimed at the defender's chin.

Still holding the right arm, the defender stomps forward slamming the length of his right arm against the attacker's left shoulder and rib cage, neutralising the energy in his punch. At the same time he engages attacker's leg bridge, breaking his support plane.

2. *Then re-converts into a double forearm neck brace.*

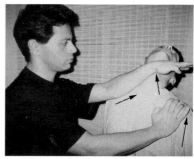

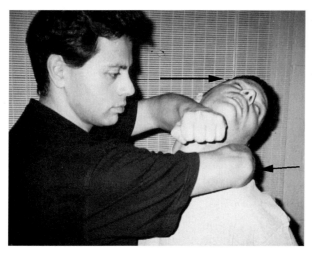

3. *Defender controls the right shoulder, simultaneously pivoting his left elbow to the shoulder. His wrist turns the attacker's head backwards and left to expose the neck.*

1. *Defender converts his grab into a double palm head hold with potential damaging consequences to the attacker's neck.*

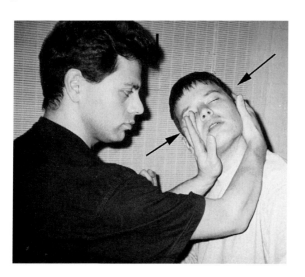

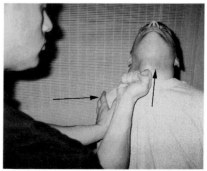

4. *Grabbing attacker's shoulder, defender delivers an accelerated phoenix eye strike to the neck.*

The Triune Brain

The human brain has evolved from 'the inside out'. Today neuro-physiologists, scientists who study the brain, identify three distinctive 'brains' based on our shared evolutionary heritage with other species. The oldest part, the brain stem and spinal cord, is known as the reptilian brain or 'R' complex. This is the seat of the instincts outlined above, and when we humans act on these ancient patterns of dominance, territoriality, aggression and sex, then we behave just like a crocodile. Deep inside us it seems, is the living, breathing brain of a dinosaur! Next, is the paleo-mammalian or 'old mammal brain'. This we share with all mammal species, and includes such structures as the limbic system, which is involved in the regulation of the major emotions, such as fear. Also included are the hypothalamus and pituitary gland, which regulate the body's endocrine or hormonal system. Also at this level, is the oldest part of the cerebral cortex; the paleo-cortex. Animals with only this level of brain development are still successful and evolutionarily viable, although they lack the higher cognitive functions associated with the next level.

Lastly comes the neo-mammalian or 'new mammal brain'. This we share with all higher mammals, except for the specifically human developments, particularly in the pre-frontal area of the cortex. At this level, all human functions and behaviours; biological, psychological and social are integrated.

It's obvious how learning that by-passes cognitive overloading, and relies instead on trained reactions that are close to instinct, will work efficiently. There are some problems however with this emphasis.

Integrative Learning - the Human Response

As a starting point, I agree wholeheartedly with the self-protection movement that relying on the development of fine-tuned motor (movement) skills, so typical of the traditional martial arts, may put people at a disadvantage in a 'live' street confrontation. However, what I advocate, based on my own 33 years training, and my very practical street experience in the police, is that starting with the self-protection approach is a great preparation or even a 'stop-gap', until serious martial arts students

---

acquire the trained ability to integrate their responses appropriately at all levels of brain function. This is precisely why I support the self-protection approach for beginning students or for people only interested in self **defence. However, for the development of advanced martial art skills, the use of the fully human cortex, with its integrative learning skills is required.**

A Charter for Psychopathy?

A second and morally more serious issue I have with the self-protection approach, is the potential for it to be hijacked and seriously misused, by violent, psychopathic personalities who may attempt to justify just about any extreme of violence against other human beings.

Some literature, purporting to originate from people connected with the self-protection approach, advocates extreme violence, and then gives quasi-legal advice on how to justify your actions in a court of law. Of course, such advice could be seen as 'self-protection' in itself, particularly given fear inducing accounts of violent attacks and law courts acquitting offenders. However, as we have seen, fear is a great persuader, and any idea however irrational may be successfully tacked-on to such beliefs. Also, the suggestion that a particular method or approach is the answer to ' fear" will be very attractive. Medical hypnotherapists understand through daily clinical practice that irrational fear is best 'disregarded' through positive self-hypnosis, and/or through a realistic appraisal of the feared situation. People who overcome true fear of a 'phobic' intensity, do so not by continuously re-exposing themselves to feared, or fear inducing situations (which may simply act as a fear-fix) but by re-framing their internal modelling of fearful situations and their sense of control over consequences.

One of the clinical features of psychopathy is a lack of true conscience, although many psychopaths are clever enough to be able to give a workable impression of having one. This is the danger of advocating the 'preemptive strike'. Although absolutely valid for self-defence, it can be made to appear justifiable on the flimsiest of grounds. Beware of people who glory in violence, or who say that they just had to do it, the dividing line between them and psychopathy may only be a **matter of**

context; witness the personality disorder units of any of Britain's top-security hospitals, or the actions of individuals involved in 'ethnic cleansing' and genocide. Some of the most dangerous psychopathic killers present themselves publicly as 'nice' people, so nice in fact that they're still smiling when they murder innocent and defenceless people.

Martial artists need to get a proper grip on this issue, and accept their responsibilities to wider society and humanity as a whole. Violent street-fighters and killers should not be acceptable role models; on the contrary, they should be resisted and rejected. Let's hope that the current 'fashion' for advocating extreme violence ends with the twentieth century: the most violent thus far in the history of the human species.

Self-protection can be a challenge and a catalyst. On the more positive side, the self-protection movement has a very useful part to play in challenging the traditional martial arts to change to meet the times, or to deservedly go under. Ideally, this movement will act as a catalyst for generative change, as the traditional arts realise that they should embrace the message, even if not the method. I believe that Peter Consterdine and Geoff Thompson have a unique role to play in this transformation, as leading advocate of the best of the self-protection systems.

The combined style is an example of integrative learning. The combat principles of the combined Hop-Gar Mantis style (see above) are such that they foster efficient integrative learning (as witnessed by my students), firstly by cutting down on the computation necessary to react, and then by releasing the appropriate responses. The acquisition of such skill is neither quick nor easy, but once attained elevates the levels of learning from instinct to intelligence.

We are fully human, and therefore we should strive to fully utilise our human heritage. Traditional arts that either have no efficient principles or have lost their meaning, need revision.

People who train in the Hop-Gar Mantis style get the best of tradition, with the very best that the western disciplines of science and philosophy have to offer.

The ethics of the martial code can be considered in relation to 'reality'. **In today's climate, talk of a martial arts code of ethics is becoming unpopular almost to the degree of being politically incorrect.** The fact that many systems forms start with a defensive 'block' is mocked for un-realism, as is the idea that martial artists should not attack first. Much of the new 'attitude' comes from people who claim superior experience in 'real' street confrontations, usually as night club doormen.

My 'real' experience comes from 13 years Police service in Merseyside, one of the toughest forces in Britain. In that arena, you meet the broadest possible range of human experiences, the good, as well as the bad and the ugly! Often you work isolated and alone, and yet are required to uphold the rule of law. If the Police 'back down' then society as a whole has 'lost-it'.

The Police are accountable under the law for their actions, which is entirely as it should be. This means that as a Police Officer, you always have to bear in mind the legal, and human, consequences of your actions. I found that this dovetailed perfectly with the traditional codes of ethics of the oriental martial arts. **Yes, I did use preemptive strikes on occasion, but the principle of minimal force under the law, was always applied;** and I had to be able to justify my actions ethically and not merely quasi-legally (see below).

As I mentioned earlier in this book, I was attacked many times in my career, by all manner of people, armed, unarmed, singly and by groups. I was hospitalised with head injuries, attacked with knives and petrol bombs and faced the threat of firearms. I also had occasion to arrest violent doormen who had 'pre-empted' me with a vicious attack. Being a 'bouncer' is not in itself something to be proud of. Yes, being a martial artist: but to achieve that means much more than advocating violence. If martial arts students want to get 'real' experience of the streets, they could no better than joining the Police. There, you would need to face human reality in all of its manifestations, and do so ethically, and responsibly.

Real ethical experience is not just about the pressure testing of physical skills, it is also about the development of character, and actions that support the common good. **Police service tests people like no other arena of human life.** Yes, there are bad and corrupt police officers (thankfully a tiny minority), but it should be remembered that the most effective resistance against bad police officers comes from the good ones, people who would lay down their lives for a stranger.

Note the use of blocks and the role of the battle computer. The use of passive blocking is easy to dismiss, as it apparently achieves nothing. Like everything else however, it depends on context. In the combined style, blocks are in the main 'active' in that they strike at pressure points, and/or source-of-movement referents. These are the major leverage or fulcrum points on the body. The main ones are quite simply the shoulders and the hips: points 11, 1, 5 and 7 on the body clock. It's very difficult to articulate or deliver 'power' if these points are struck or controlled. **My Mantis teachers always emphasised 'taking an attack out 'at source'.** Of course, the ultimate source is the attackers brain! However, if you are forced to react swiftly 'from cold' then these major joints are very practical options. Experienced attackers usually ensure that their head/chin is well covered, but few expect the pain and shock of a penetrative joint destruction attack on their punching arm.

Constant 'quality' training, and the refinement of technique, as an advanced higher-brain skill, means that these interceptions work cleanly and efficiently. This of course is the 'battle computer" mentioned in the Principles chapter. The pressure testing of these methods, means that the computer eventually functions without conscious thought, but purely through the rapid process of: perception; targeting, range, engagement with speed and power, leading to the destruction of the opponents attack.

If you remember the role of the aircraft carrier escorts in the Falklands war, their function was to act as 'goal-keepers', to shoot down incoming enemy aircraft or missiles, that were attacking the carriers. The escorts battle computers would only 'protect' their own ship however, so the escorting frigates had to sail as closely as possible to the carrier, so that any attack on them, would be computed as an attack on the frigate. In effect, the carriers handed over the responsibility for their defence, to the escorts' computers.

In the combined style, the carriers would be the conscious personality, and the escort the trained 'battle computer'. This distinction, shows how to limit or eliminate the so-called 'log-jam' effect, wherein the conscious mind is overwhelmed by the need to choose from a huge range of techniques or responses, and in effect either fails to react or reacts inappropriately. **The battle computer is a higher-brain cognitive map and processor, that incorporates instinctive reactions, but acts principally through intelligently trained experience.** Like the escort frigates, it functions with relative independence from conscious control, and is therefore less vulnerable to distraction or overloading.

The reaction all depends on the level of threat, which is re-assessed moment by moment. If the threat develops then so does the response, all in accordance with the styles guiding principles; which is in effect the battle computers programming.

Kicks and Leg-manoeuvres

The use of kicks in the street is yet another controversial area. Many 'practical' martial artists advise that only low or even 'very low' kicks should ever be used. Some add that groin kicks are likely to be ineffective and are best avoided. From a 'system' point of view, the combined Hop- Gar Mantis utilises the full range of kicks, combined with hand techniques, footwork and the use of the legs for 'ramming and jamming'. There is no dogma about the rights and wrongs of height or target; there doesn't have to be, as the style is 'principle led'. **Kicks as such, are opportunistic, but never de-contextualised.**

As for groin kicks, in my Police career I have found them to be effective. Firstly, as direct strikes, appropriate in a given situation; and secondly as 'warning shots'. In these instances, a very fast front snap kick at the groin of an attacker who is closing from a sufficient distance to be discouraged without contact proved to be effective. Most street attackers don't expect that kind of response from a uniformed Police Officer. As a simple and direct strategy, I found it to be very workable, even where the attacker was not put-off. It either broke their concentration enough to allow me to close the range on my own terms, or allowed me to 'release' a stream of stop-hit style interceptions, and if required, 'finishing' techniques. **A favourite of mine was the close hook kick to the groin impacting with the toes.** This is a very surprising hit, that can be launched from an upright clinch position, even whilst moving or being pushed, backwards. It also has the advantage of a natural chambering for 'leg-bar' techniques, engaging the hips at either 5 or 7 O'clock on the transverse hip plane.

Other useful kicking or leg techniques include balance breaking strikes through the hips or support plane; 'masked treads' (covered by verbal distraction and/or hand techniques), or traps to the feet and lower leg; Using toe kicks with heavy duty footwear to the ankles, whilst slipping a punch or an attempt at grappling can also be effective. The same toe-kick hooked into the inner thigh above the knee was effective, as this struck on a 'wobble point' (if the opponent's weight was transferring through that leg) and also a nerve pressure point.

Kicks at the knee and the shin where effective 'discouragers' or 'distractors' but usually not enough in themselves to stop a determined attack. Again it all depends on context, and your battle-computer's ability to manage the situations at the right level and rate of response. **I never found kicks with the knee particularly effective, at least for me.** They seemed difficult to 'set-up' and to be more like a ritualised action, rather than a clean technique. I did find kicks with the shin to be useful however, especially when dropping weight into an attacker. Overall, if things 'kicked-off' so to speak, I preferred to use my feet for mobility, positioning and balance; also as platforms for ramming, jamming, and for hand techniques. In combination with the above however they had their definite uses.

Elbow Strikes

Elbow strikes are probably one of the most misunderstood and misapplied techniques for street applications. Critics say that you never get a chance for a clean elbow strike, or that they are 'telegraphic'. Of course, if you adopt the 'stand-off' chamber and deliver approach, with the assumption that your target obligingly stands still, then yes they are telegraphic! In my experience, elbows, like kicks, are best used opportunistically. This means that the specific circumstances of the situation, plus your system's guiding principles, determine their use.

Please don't let technique determine your response!   If you do you may as well be in a world of your own, as you're not switched on to what's going on in front of your face. I certainly found elbows to be effective in the Police.   Obviously, because of their potential to cause damage, I had to use them carefully, for example: as stop hitting 'discouragers' i.e. destruction techniques, on the limbs against kicks or over extended punches; as fulcrums for grappling; as contact hits against the shoulder, to spin that attacker into a more accessible position; and as 'concealed' finishers, launched from very close range against the jaw. In the combined style, there is a much wider range of elbow techniques, but thankfully I never had need of their use as some are frankly lethal.

Pressure Point and Meridian Strikes

These too are controversial.   Once again I have to say that **I found pressure point strikes most effective in my Police career,** as any strike to a pressure point imparts a greater response than say a flat fist or a palm on to a muscular or bony area. However, I wish to re-emphasise that I am not referring to so-called 'meridian strikes', but to anatomically vulnerable parts of the body and the associated psychological response to pain and to control (see below under Meridian Striking; Chi or Cheat?).

As a first principle, the amount of energy or force applied must always be within the law, and justifiable on the ethical grounds established in the traditions of the martial arts.   However, the precise amount of force required will vary, and cannot be known with any certainty in advance.

The combined Hop-Gar Mantis system teaches the use of multiple striking against whatever vital and/or control points present themselves opportunistically. This means without the need for planning by the martial artist, or compliance by the attacker. The impact force and effect of a given blow is not limited simply to the momentum of its delivery. It also includes the amount of force applied per unit of contact area in the striking weapon (e.g. a single knuckle fist); the position and movement of the target and its vulnerability to damage.

What proves to be lethal force against one body target may have little effect against another. Alternatively, slight impactive force in the right place can disable or paralyse. Multiple hits based on good target computation will increase effective results. Beyond force however, there is the very important role of the mind and brain in interpreting or 'making sense' of being struck.

Mind Matters

We have seen that multiple strikes increase the probability of success, as more targets are engaged and stimulated. This stimulation can be cumulative so that it produces an overload effect on the brain of the attacker, leading to a trance-like state of resignation, and defeat. The blows may be very forceful, or even slight. The key to the overloaded trance state response is the meaning placed on stimulation and pain by the attacker's brain. This meaning has many contributing factors including instinct, conditioning, social scenario and perhaps most importantly suggestion.

The instinct to 'give-up' when overwhelmed runs very deep, and can be witnessed most clearly in prey animals when finally cornered by a predator, for example an African zebra brought down by a lion. At such times the prey almost 'relaxes into its fate'. Human beings do the same thing, at the point when they feel death is near or to struggle is pointless, the human mind dissociates from what is happening, and exhibiting a pseudo-calmness.

Even where death is not perceived as imminent, people still dissociate for protective purposes. In everyday life we might say that the person 'froze'. In combat, we can see people go rigid with shock and or pain. The net result is the same. It is an inability to respond due to overloading, in effect, a trance.

Conditioning can produce the same effect through simple learning and expectation. This is at the heart of the compliance found in martial arts training, particularly in the influence of instructors over students. The student has learned to produce the expected outcomes, on demand.

The influence of social situation or scenario is important as there are implicit rules of behaviour and response 'built in'. We all acquire these rules, unconsciously, and then limit our responses in accordance with what is appropriate to the given social situation. If you know how to read the rules, you can manipulate them, as any competent hypnotist knows.

Suggestion

This brings us to 'suggestion', the common linking factor in all of the above. Essentially suggestion is about influence. This can arise from instincts which operate automatically from our past learning (which includes training), and from the rules of social interaction. Suggestion, linked to the utilisation of naturally occurring trance states, is the key to all effective hypnosis, and it should come as no surprise that we find its active use in the teaching of vital and pressure point striking in the martial arts.

Meridian striking - Chi or Cheat ?

Some martial arts authorities, particularly those involved in claims of meridian striking, state that very slight force is necessary to obtain the desired result. They may further suggest the use of a 'force-multiplier' which involves the 'stimulation' of multiple meridian points, in order to overwhelm an attacker through the application of minimal force or expenditure of energy.

There is no doubt that there are very real effects to these supposed meridian strikes. However, the attribution of these effects to energy channels based on acupuncture and traditional Chinese medicine has absolutely no basis whatsoever in scientifically validated research. The suggestion that they are based on secret traditional knowledge carries enormous psychological influence and power, particularly with western martial arts students, whose social conditioning and prior learning leads them to expect an effect.

Where many fall down on understanding this phenomenon is in believing that they themselves are rational and sceptical individuals, who actually don't believe in all this mystical stuff about Chi and pressure points, and the rest. The point here is that it is not their conscious beliefs about themselves that are decisive, but their unconscious suggestibility which is very often equal and opposite to their stated and honestly held opinions. This is how stage-hypnotism works, on the unconscious, not on what people say or believe about themselves. In clinical hypnosis, it is well known that people who claim to be the most rational or most resistant are often the easiest to hypnotise.

Clinically, a good hypnotherapist will utilise a person's beliefs to 'coat' the delivery of suggestions, which then will be accepted as they are hidden within something that appears reasonable and believable. In the case of 'Masters' of meridian striking, such people may be expert manipulators of what are in effect very carefully controlled situations, which have their implicit social rules, and therefore inevitable results. Alternatively, they may be decent and honest people who actually believe what they are saying themselves, and then convincingly communicate those beliefs to others, so that all share in what is in effect a mutual suggestion.

The effects generated by meridian strikes can be explained by reference to known anatomical weak points on the body, the 'overloading effect' on the brain and mind; and by suggestion. Any worthwhile stage hypnotist could produce the same results in a group of martial arts students, simply by observing the 'rules' of interaction between Master and student. All that would then be necessary is that the students should believe that the hypnotist is a 'Master' and the rest they would do to themselves.

In the mid-nineteenth century, hypnosis came to prominence as a medical treatment for an apparently bizarre condition known as hysteria. This involved the production of a whole host of physical and mental symptoms that had no organic or physical cause. And yet, the sufferers produced real symptoms including such things as loss of sensation and movement in limbs (paralysis). It was found that the key was the sufferers' unconscious idea of paralysis, and not the true effects of trauma or nerve damage. The body simply reproduced what the mind believed.

The medical hypnotists of the day were able to demonstrate the power of suggestion to remove these symptoms altogether, and even to replace them with entirely new and unrelated ones. They were also able to induce hysteria in normal healthy people, thereby proving that humans are universally vulnerable to suggestion and influence. Many of the results of claimed meridian strikes at seminars are literally hysterical, and would be recognised as such by qualified medical hypnotists.

The 'idea' of Chi and meridian channels is sufficient to produce an effect if appropriately believed in. Naturally these effects will not appear to follow known western medical knowledge, and will therefore appear even more powerful to people who have been educated by society to believe in the power of western medicine. A way of 'coating' suggestions of meridian effects to a western audience could involve the 'dressing-up' of eastern mysticism with western science, thereby making the sugar-pill of suggestion easier to swallow, and indeed some martial artists on the 'meridian striking seminar circuit' do just that. The power of auto-suggestion is so great that sometimes it can even work against a person when he is specifically told that their is nothing mystical about pressure point striking and that it is all based on physics, anatomy and suggestion.

Recently I was approached by a Dan graded (Black Belt) Karate-ka. He stated that he wanted to learn the Praying Mantis system because of its pressure point techniques. I specifically told him of my position, and agreed to demonstrate for him on some of my senior instructors.

His 'unconscious belief' was so insistent, that **despite my efforts at explanation he produced bruising, swellings and tenderness on his body, without his even being touched!** He telephoned me a couple of days later, and was quite convinced that he had been secretly touched or that Chi had been 'projected' into him at a distance. This is an example of a clinical hysteria, and although I made every effort to explain the position and to educate him, he is in all probability still very vulnerable to suggestion to this day.

This example highlights the importance of unconscious belief, as this man's training was no defence whatsoever against auto-suggestion. He had arrogantly asserted that he would be able to resist any attempt made by anyone to influence him through hypnosis as he was so rational and so very well educated. Events proved he was mistaken.

The key factors then involve suggestion and unconscious belief. Some of the meridian striking seminar circuit instructors are decent people, who honestly believe in what they are teaching. Others are frankly charlatans. However, In the 'real world' of street self defence, it is far better to put your money on scientifically validated knowledge, otherwise the reverse feedback effect of failure will be devastating... perhaps even fatal.

What are Pressure Points ?

Essentially, pressure points are areas of the body particularly vulnerable to striking or other forms of 'pressure' such as pinching, biting, squeezing, pulling, pressing or locking; simply, to attack. The effect of applying force to these points varies. The key is of course accessibility. There's no point in struggling to get at a particular point if ten others are wide open!   Sometimes, striking or controlling a given point actually opens up access to others, as a kind of natural progression.

How are the effects caused ? This depends on the point or points in question. The first thing to appreciate is the role of the nervous system in registering   pain.   Pain is understood by the World Health Organisation (WHO) as both a physical and a psychological phenomenon.

On the physical level, pressure points have a good and responsive supply of specialised nerve receptor cells known as nociceptors (pain receptors), which function to signal actual or potential tissue damage to the brain. Related nerve cell receptors include mechanoreceptors (physical-pressure and de-formation receptors) and thermoreceptors (temperature and friction receptors).

Each such cell has a receptive field which if appropriately stimulated triggers a signal to the brain. In the case of pain, there are different kinds of cell fibres that communicate different kinds of pain perception such as fast pain, and slow pain. A further important distinction is between somatic and visceral pain. Somatic pain arises either from nociceptors in the skin, known as superficial somatic pain, or from receptors in the skeletal muscles, joints, tendons and other connective tissues, which is referred to as deep somatic pain.

Visceral pain results from stimulation of pain receptors in the major organs. Superficial somatic pain will elicit a good response in an attacker, as the human body as evolved to 'consider' the skin as its first line of defence against the environment. However, non-lethal disabling strikes usually require the stimulation of deep somatic pain, via muscle, joint or bone tissue. As we saw in the 'Principles' chapter above, designer attacks on bone and muscle are very effective as there is no additional layer of protective anatomical tissue, in effect they are armour piercing shots !

The brain makes sense of the location of pain in an area known as the somatosensory cortex, a strip of brain material that runs like an 'Alice Band' from each side and over the top of the head. This acts as a kind of map of the body. Further meaning is made by the cerebral cortex (the brain's two hemispheres) as a whole. It is at this level that psychology comes into play.

The psychology of pain perception is complex, but it involves all the factors discussed above such as instinct, conditioning, social context and suggestion. There is also the role of analgesia (repression or lack of pain) that comes into play during emergencies. This is usually a combination of psychological dissociation (splitting off from the experience) and the release of opioid (natural opiates) substances that function as pain killers.

Some people have higher natural tolerances to pain, or even a specific condition known as congenital analgesia. This is an inherited condition which can lead to the complete absence of pain perception. Another rare condition or state, is synesthesia within which different perceptions can be transformed into one another. Usually this involves things like the 'hearing of colours' or the 'smell of sounds'. Sometimes however, pain itself is transformed into something else, and in effect no longer signals actual or potential tissue damage.

None of the above actually prevents tissue damage, only its perception. This is why it is important to utilise the body's natural control points (as in the body-clock) as well as the pressure point strikes themselves.

The issue of non-responders is interesting, and in my experience such people who attend as students on the seminar circuit are probably either synesthetics, or have a good level of negative-suggestibility that is, a base-line resistance to the unwarranted effects of harmful suggestion. Of course the seminar instructors don't see it that way. They would rather try to explain it in terms of Chi and meridian channels yet again, as that would support the rest of what they do. This is a useful trick, to be able to explain failure in terms of the suggestions that you deliver. It's the same sort of thing that is employed by stage hypnotists!

What about Vital Points?

Vital points are a special sub-class of pressure points, and generally refer to strikes or blows to areas that have potentially lethal consequences. Naturally, pain perception is a factor, but not so important, as the effect of a successful vital point attack transcends pain and directly threatens life itself. Essentially, such blows must compromise either/or the brain and the heart. Both may be attacked directly, or just as effectively indirectly, via blood vessels or major nerves controlling say respiration or heart rate.

Often, pressure and vital point attacks can summate (add-up) to a fatal outcome. There are some very serious ethical, moral and legal issues here, particularly when it is appreciated just how easily a person can be killed, even accidentally.

What about pressure point knock outs? These are a favourite of the seminar circuit, and of the popular imagination. 'Knock-outs' as understood in western boxing involve loss of consciousness due to compression and shearing forces acting on the brain, or to loss of respiratory function and therefore the supply of oxygen after being 'winded'. The 'martial arts' type of knockout via pressure point striking is often due to sophisticated versions of the aforementioned. However, the martial arts are also adept at occluding blood vessels by strangulation and striking, and can 'arrest' the heart of an attacker by compression of the sternum (breast bone) Other similar techniques abound, but the supposed meridian channel knock-outs are most often 'stunning' actions, caused by a mixture of pain perception, central nervous system 'overloading', social-context and auto-suggestion.

Hypnotists can 'knock people out' simply by using words, no physical contact is necessary. They can even do so indirectly whilst talking to another person. Hypnosis can work covertly without the 'subject' knowing what is happening, and hypnotists can and do hypnotise people against their will. The hypnotic influence could easily be seen as occult or magical, and indeed the oldest explanation for its effect is a 'subtle magnetic energy' (Mesmerism) similar to Chi (see above). However, the real effects of hypnosis are understood.   Suggestion directly affects the brain, the endocrine system, even the immune system; all real psycho-physiological pathways. The amount of control and even predictability of results in hypnosis arises from these very real mind-body interactive systems.   Meridian strikes work by the same pathways, not by the manipulation of chi flowing along invisible, non physical channels.

When it comes to considering the 'healing' effects of so-called chi energy, then I am prepared to consider it, but only because its effects can be replicated using other names (such as western spiritual healing or Mesmerism) and because of the results of 'double blind' scientific trials in the United States, that controlled for the possible affects of suggestion, showed a statistically significant clinical effect (see above).   Such biofield effects can therefore be demonstrated in healing, but don't require the unnecessary trappings and suggestion of chi and meridians. Many will say that what can be used to heal can be used to harm. Perhaps.   However, it should be noted that **the healing effects of acupuncture (on which theory much of meridian striking is based) are yet to be convincingly demonstrated scientifically beyond analgesia (pain relief).** In analgesia it seems that far from acting on meridians, the needles whether manually rotated or electrically stimulated, work directly on nerve pathways, and encourage the secretion of endorphins (the body's natural pain killers).   The analgesic effects of acupuncture can easily be matched by hypnosis. In the mid 19th century, surgi-

The Evolutionary Cycle of Change in Martial Arts Systems

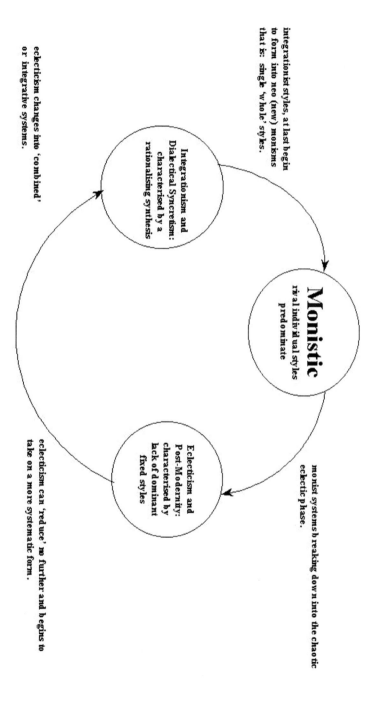

Integrationism and Dialectical Syncretism: characterised by a rationalising synthesis

Monistic
rival individual styles predominate

Eclecticism and Post-Modernity: characterised by lack of dominant fixed styles

monist systems breaking down into the chaotic eclectic phase.

eclecticism can 'reduce' no further and begins to take on a more systematic form.

eclecticism changes into 'combined' or integrative systems.

integrationist styles, at last begin to form into neo (new) monisms that is: single 'whole' styles.

The evolutionary cycle of cultural change in martial arts systems, starting with 'monist' or single dominant styles; which then break down during an eclectic, chaotic, or 'post-modern phase' (as in the late 20th century) This will eventually generate an integrative or 'syncretistic' phase, which itself will go on to produce a new or neo-monist stage, characterised by the creation of yet more 'single' or whole, styles. In the history of human culture, all systems endlessly repeat this elementary cyclical process, as a basis for generative change.

(C) 1995 Steve Richards.

cal operations were routinely carried out by British doctors working in India. Even amputations with no pain control other than Mesmerism!

The other so-called healing effects of acupuncture may be explained through the power of the mind and body to work in concert to heal itself, if permission is given in the right way, and in the right situation. Current scientific research into psycho-biological hypnosis in the United States is identifying the real processes at work in such healing. If the supportive theory for acupuncture were correct, then it would be possible to eliminate disease and death purely by its use to balance the hypothesised energies. This hasn't happened, and if and when it does, it is much more likely to be through advances in scientific micro-biology and genetics.

As for the harmful effects, these are likely to be through suggestion, which as any informed occultist knows can kill efficiently, quickly and even at a pre-determined rate. Most 'Voodoo' deaths are caused this way, supplemented by poisons such as tetrotodoxin (Puffer-Fish poison) which is a nerve agent that can simulate death, leading to a belief in 'Zombies'.

I have written in detail on this area, in order to encourage martial artists to be aware of what is really going on, and hopefully to avoid the possibility of discrediting real pressure point striking by negative association to fanciful beliefs in meridians. There are very real effects, but, the attribution of their cause to meridians is misleading. How much more progress could be made if science and suggestion were properly understood!

I would advise martial artists to better educate themselves on real scientific anatomy and physiology, and to get some effective training in hypnosis. Apply these to an efficient traditional system that strikes mechanically at real targets and you will get the desired effects. No need for dressing things up in metaphysics or quasi-oriental bull-shit.

Padded Clothing and the Targeting of Pressure Points

This is a very real consideration, particularly if you limit your approach to 'light contact strikes' on very specific points. Also, single knuckle hits, which are a favoured delivery system in Hop-Gar Mantis, are sometimes reduced in effect by padding, rather like the effect of a bullet proof vest However, there are other options. Many very workable pressure points lie on the 'Sam-Gwan' (see above) on the arms and legs and on the body-clock control points. All of these are amenable to direct force, as in applied Newtonian mechanics, and can effectively unbalance an attacker, despite padding in the form of leathers or even 'designer' protective clothing. This breaking of an attackers balance and/or momentum, is perfectly valid as a set-up for following techniques, including grappling. On the floor, padding is a disadvantage, as I know from years of wearing unwieldy Police uniforms! Even crash helmets need not be too much of a problem. They can act as very efficient 'long-levers' to exert great 'compelling force' to an attacker. Remember, destruction techniques are part of an overall package, and should be utilised as appropriate. Destruction as a principle, refers to the destruction of an attack (see Principles chapter) which may or may not need to include such specifically named techniques.

Pre-emptive Strikes

All Kung-Fu systems incorporate these techniques, but they are often not contextualised sufficiently by teachers. In part this is due to the very right and proper consideration of ethical issues, and in part due sadly to ignorance and lack of ability. There is a very fine line between making the right and wrong choices over this issue, and the stakes are high either way. I believe that on balance, students must be taught to be able to react pre-emptively, but that this also must be tempered by the teacher. This is his/her responsibility, as the student may have a latent violent psychopathic personality disorder, or due to fear induced suggestion may find him/her self programmed to react in the 'Roman fashion' (attack is the best form of defence) even in unwarrantable circumstances.

In the Police, I was often pre-empted by an attacker, particularly whilst gaining in experience, and also as I was mindful of the consequences should I 'lose it' and work-out on the other person. I remember on one occasion, whilst trying to defuse a situation with an enraged night club bouncer. I smiled at him and put both hands in my pockets to show I was not threatening him. **The next thing I remembered was flying through the air, like in a Tom & Jerry cartoon, and sliding down a wall.** I did secure his arrest, but it was probably the hardest hit I'd taken up to that time, and it made me re-think my approach. I was lucky that he had caught me on the cheek, rather than on the chin!

On other occasions, I had to make a very quick decision and just go for it. Once, a female colleague and I found ourselves confronting a deranged youth whom we believed was armed with a hunting knife, following a stabbing at a local club. The Policewoman was standing between me and the youth, near the edge of a motorway flyover. It was at night, and I had to make a quick decision. If he pulled a weapon and went for her, she'd probably be stabbed. If I moved closer to him, he may panic and pull the knife anyway. I was young only nineteen years of age and decided to go for it. I pushed the Policewoman out of the way, and struck him on the side of the jaw, his legs buckled, but he stood up and put his hand inside his jacket. I was now within grappling distance and I ended up dangling him over the bridge. This encouraged him to give-up!

Another knife incident, this time at a domestic dispute, involved a decision to close the range against a knife attack in order to get my hit in first. I was asked by a woman occupier to remove her violent live-in boyfriend, who had been threatening to kill her. Again, this was at night, in the early hours, and I had been on duty for a long time. My concentration was lower than I would have liked, but working in a constant state of fatigue was routine on Police shifts.

I told the man to leave and he replied 'outside?' to which I said yes, not realising at that point that this was a challenge to fight, outside! I saw him go into the kitchen, which normally would have made me very suspicious, but he came out again quickly and headed for the front door. I followed him to make sure he left the premises, but once outside he produced a kitchen knife and began swinging it at me. I realised that I was so close to him that I must go forward; to go backwards would be a serious error, as this would encourage him to come forward aggressively. I caught the next knife swing by passing inside the arc of his arm and punched him to the ground. Fortunately, I had heavy Police clothing on, and the knife harmlessly 'slapped' against my back. Not the most ideal of reactions on my part. But on this occasion forwards was better than backwards.

Months later, when awaiting his trial, I received a note from the prosecutions department stating that he had 'been bailed to 'a higher court', a Police euphemism for him being dead. It seems that he took his own life whilst awaiting the trial. Something to think about here as people who harm themselves in that ultimate way are sometimes willing to kill others, without conscience.

Some pre-emptive strikes arose out of developing situations, that perhaps could not have been escalated safely at their beginning. I remember one of the many situations in which I was cornered by a drunken gang and was about to be attacked, when assistance chanced to pass by, and the gang dissipated. Common Police practice was to let the situation go, in the belief that it had effectively sorted itself out. However, I was determined to arrest one of the gang who had been the chief trouble maker. I approached him from behind and having observed that he was right handed, placed my right hand on his left shoulder, in order to encourage him to turn to face me with his weaker side leading. He stopped, turned around, snarled and went to punch me with his now 'isolated' right fist. I could have avoided or blocked the punch, but then his mates were still around and I knew that if he was going to fight that I would have to drop him quickly. As he turned, his centre line opened-up and I planted a front snap kick straight in his testicles which pole-axed him to the floor. I count this as an example of a pre-emptive strike, because his actions were threatening rather than fully developed. Still it had the desired effect. His mates were stunned psychologically by what they saw happen, and I effected the arrest appropriately.

Sometimes, I was forced to create an opportunity for pre-emptive strikes, by encouraging potentially violent individuals to commit themselves. On occasion, potential street disorder situations will diffuse in the presence of the Police, only to re-ignite more dangerously when they have gone. At these times you have to decide if it's wiser to goad dangerous persons into committing themselves to attack, in order to save potential harm to innocent people later on. An elementary understanding of posturing and attack rituals, typical of any baboon or monkey troupe, are enough to size up and manage such a situation; nothing more sophisticated is necessary. However, once committed, you have to take them out efficiently. This is a gray legal area, but practical Police experience supports its necessary use. I know that any experienced Police Officer will understand what I mean.

Grappling

My experience of practical Police work supports the notion that grappling is an integral part of street confrontations. However, in my Police service, I found that more often than not grappling was an option used by drunken or otherwise disorientated aggressors, who couldn't maintain enough balance and co-ordination to punch or kick effectively.

As a Policeman, I found grappling and restraint to be most useful in overcoming half serious, ritualised resistance to arrest scenarios. Other than that, as a finisher following a more serious blow by blow fight. Most attackers seemed unwilling to be on the floor themselves, as if it's an almost natural reaction to want to re-gain the upright position. Fortunately, I never fought with an expert grappler on the ground in the street, only in training! (see above for the Hop-Gar Mantis approach to grappling).

The Flaws in Police Self-Defence Training

This is a topic for a book all of its own! **Police training in the 70's and 80's was pathetic and abysmally unreal, pandering to what today**

---

would be called political correctness. I remember being on night duty and talking to a young colleague who was enthralled by his Taiho-Jitsu training, and wanting to show me how I couldn't get out of his arrest holds. He said to try anything so confident was he in the propaganda that he had been sold. I suppose that I took on the dubious responsibility of re-educating him, and hopefully by example saving him from his false sense of security. His 'technique' required compliance in order to apply it and then isolation of one wrist and arm, so that any attempt to turn into the hold produced pain and increased effectiveness of the lock. However it required him to walk forwards and to one side in a circular way.

Like a lot of people who are preoccupied with hands, he forgot the feet, and tripped over my foot which I passively placed in his path. As he stumbled his grip weakened and I belted him on his helmeted head, sharply, with my Police issue torch. The shock to this very nice young officer nearly brought him to tears. But, it helped to bring him to his senses. It's a shame that the people who have to face the most fearsome of street situations, on behalf of us members of the public, have little beyond courage and resolve to help them, having been misled by the 'politically correct' into accepting nonsensical self-defence training.

Multiple Strikes

Again many 'authorities' say that the use of multiple strikes, or anything apparently more complicated than a basic combination, is unworkable on the street. I suppose it all depends upon your knowledge and experience. If you don't know how to do it then they may be right.

In fact, very few systems teach anything like the necessary skills to be able to deliver multiple hits cleanly and efficiently. It all boils down to appropriate perceptive and motor skills training and proper targeting computation.

Some practical street fighters champion the single 'big hit', and quite validly justify this by saying that it maybe the only chance you get, so get yours in first and quickly. **I can go along with this up to a point**, but the problem is that you may not have sufficient control over the consequences of landing say a knock-out punch to the chin. In my Police career, **I attended at least two cases of manslaughter, where the 'victim' had been felled in the street by a single punch, but died from the 'secondary impact' of his head on the floor.** The legal judgement in these cases held that there was no proof of intent to kill (murder) but manslaughter (the unintentional but unlawful killing of another person) is still punishable by life imprisonment. It's not possible beforehand to know the health or fitness status of an attacker. This may seem a ludicrous thing to consider, but if in our enthusiasm we strike someone with a thin skull or a heart condition, then reasonable force may suddenly become a manslaughter charge!

Complex multiple strikes, delivered rapidly to different parts of the body, certainly have the potential to cause lethal harm. They also increase in effect through a kind of 'force multiplier' However, they have one major advantage over the single big hit artillery option and that is flexibility of response. Please don't mistake this for weakness of response. **Where multiple strikes impact on pressure and control points they have great stopping power, and remove options for follow up from the attacker.** Also on a psychological level, they prepare the practitioner for a rapid fire engagement against a determined attack. The big hit option has less follow up potential as a technique.

In the Police I remember working with a very hard ex-paratrooper, who was skilled in boxing, and had served in Northern Ireland. We were engaged in a car chase around the town centre, and when the driver bailed out and did a runner, my colleague, a very fit lad, sprinted after him, overcoming the advantage the other driver had in adrenalin, and effected an arrest. However, the prisoner decided he was going to get away and a struggle ensued. My colleague grappled his man on to the floor, gained the mount position, and dropped a strong full bodied right hook to the jaw. As I watched, the prisoner took the blow, grinned and said, 'Is that the best you can fucking do!'. He then shook my colleague off and started to kick the hell out of him. It took the cumulative effect of a combined multi-level pressure point attack to overpower and handcuff him. My boxing colleague's 'big hit' had no effect other than to make things worse.

Another point made against multiple hits, which is also levelled at pressure point strikes, is that in a highly aroused state, adrenalin will override pain, and the blows will be ineffective. This certainly sounds reasonable, but at least as far as the combined style is concerned, it should be remembered that pressure point strikes are usually compounded with control point impacts, in multi-strike applications. As these can be based just as much on mechanics as on anatomy, they need not rely on 'pain' for effectiveness. No matter how aroused, effective control of major joints inhibits movement, and direct blows to these sites have significant shock-stopping power.

Being an 'expert commentator' is a risky business, as there is a tendency to over-generalise from limited knowledge and experience. This is particularly true in the martial arts, wherein the range of technique is so vast and the need to understand so great. Critics of multiple strikes may believe on the basis of their own experience that they don't work. I can flatly contradict that and cite my 'real' Police experience to counterbalance any background of practicality that they may wish to quote. Even so, I am aware of the relativity of my truth compared to anyone else's and would ask the impartial reader to come to his own judgement about it.

The combined Hop-Gar Mantis system is built around principles that encourage the delivery of multiple techniques. The 'frame' for their application can be either pre-emptive or reactive, and has proven more than effective in real Police work, against dangerous and violent criminals.

Kung-Fu for the street is a matter of 'open learning', this best being achieved through 'pressure testing'. However, apart from the merely physical, ethics,ideologies and character can be pressure tested too. There's a lot of talk about the development of character in the arts, just as there is about physical ability. One without the other is unbalanced, and this achievement of balance should never be taken for granted. Some of the very finest martial artists I have ever known have been anonymous; never appearing in the pages of the martial arts media. Certainly, the most 'spiritual' people I have met have rarely been martial arts practitioners. Kung-Fu (as in any martial art) is about 'people'; their strengths and their limitations. In the end, all we can really hope to 'achieve.

Philosophy and Mental Training

'An unexamined life is not worth living' - Socrates

This chapter deals with two complementary factors, which are sadly more often talked about rather actually lived, in the martial arts. **In the popular imagination, masters of the martial arts are learned philosophers and disciplined practitioners of self-awareness. In truth however, many very senior martial artists have no philosophical education, and lack the knowledge necessary for developing a profound insight into their own psyche.** This is perhaps an unwelcome truth, but one which martial artists need to own up to, in order to grow beyond the stage of 'auto-suggestion' and even frank delusion, about their 'spiritual' or psychological development. Of course, the above picture does not apply to all martial arts masters or teachers, but it does describe enough of them in order to be a very serious issue, and one usefully addressed by students who are interested in furthering their own spiritual or psychological progress.

Philosophy in the martial arts? The term 'philosophy' is taken from the ancient Greek for 'love of wisdom'. As a discipline it has grown and developed for around three thousand years. Today, like the martial arts themselves, philosophy exists in many competing schools of thought. What many of them have in common is a concern with the truth about life, existence, and human nature.

But what of philosophy and the practice of oriental martial arts; **is there such a thing as martial arts philosophy,** and if so, is it practiced by westerners? To answer this, we should first understand that **philosophy as understood in the west is primarily about reasoning.** What we westerners interpret as philosophy in the East is more usually about an attitude towards life, tinged with arcane wisdom and perhaps religion. This is all well and good, but it is not about the same type of thinking which we find in most western philosophy, and does not produce a similar understanding. Indeed, in a negative sense, the incorporation of such ideas into the West, abstracted out their cultural origin, can even be harmful. It all depends on the individual 'soil' within which these ideas take root. **Ideas, concepts and notions, which are 'packaged' in an agreeable emotional tone, often are taken quite uncritically,** and carry substantial 'suggestive power'.

Feeling Toned Ideas and the Power of Suggestion

Some vulnerable people, who may need a direction in life or a guiding belief, may find that these influences only separate them even more from reality, and alienate them from the healing effects of normal social contact within their own culture. On a less obvious level, the effects may only be that the individuals in question develop rather strange beliefs. Harmless? Perhaps, it just depends what gets 'tacked on' to these ideas, and how they may be used to influence others.

'Feeling toned ideas' can be powerfully convincing. We are constantly told that; 'if it feels right it is right', or, 'trust your feelings'. Western type 'thinking', however, with its emphasis on analysis, is more open to reasonable debate. With a rational approach to things, the 'evidence' rather than the 'feeling' is decisive.

The beneficial effects of immersion into oriental culture are obvious, even compelling. However, the fundamental dangers hinted at above are not limited only to the importation of eastern ideas into the west; here we are just as vulnerable to 'home grown' suggestion, and in the context of the martial arts we should find evidence of this in western practitioners who may have eschewed eastern influence, in favour of something that appeals to our sense of 'practicality' or even 'reality'. This is a serious issue, as it will help in understanding the inevitable process of change involved as western culture begins to assimilate eastern martial arts. It will also shed light on the universal human predilection to suggestion.

Methods of Reasoning

There are a number of approaches to reasoning in western philosophy. The most fundamental derive from classical Greece. These are demonstrable reasoning upon which our western scientific method is based; and dialectical reasoning which employs what has been called;

'pure reason'; or reasoning as a rational on-going process, through dialogue and debate.

Demonstrable reasoning works in a practical way to show why and how things are what they are. This is the basis for the scientific method with its emphasis on controlled and repeatable experimentation, and the verification principle for any findings or conclusions. Closely related to this is the philosophical notion of empiricism. This can have a number of meanings, but in connection with the scientific method it clearly refers to factual proof of an objective kind. It does have another contextual meaning however, that of the verification of experience subjectively. This is a very important distinction, as some western martial artists claim to be 'empiricists', and may thereby imply some objective claim for the truth of their personal experiences. As we saw above, **emotionally charged personal beliefs are 'auto-suggestive' and generally not open to criticism.** The use of the validating term 'empirical' can, as a 'power-word', act to reinforce the strength of personal beliefs, and even communicate a degree of 'truth value' to others, as a kind of extension of the original auto-suggestion.

What are the limitations of the scientific method and the criteria for a truly scientific martial art? Science (from the Latin, Scientia, meaning 'knowledge') is only a tool; despite the tendency in our contemporary times to elevate it to some kind of near-religious authority. As a tool, it can be both misunderstood and misapplied. Any martial art that makes claim of being 'scientific' must qualify itself. **Science is just an experimental method used to test hypotheses or unproven theories.** Therefore, this self-critical, and self-correcting element must be present, with the art in question being capable of change and development, if the 'results' of its experimentation indicate that it should. It's no use at all trying to make the facts fit the style, or the dogma. A truly scientific style would be under continuous development. The original structure and content of the system would be a hypothesis, which would then have to be tested against the facts of experience, in a controlled and repeatable way.

However, the scientific method has some rather severe limitations. The more complex the phenomena it observes, the more difficult it is to apply. Human nature is perhaps the most complicated and multi-factorial phenomenon known. Accordingly, science as a method can only be applied with rigour to specific parts of the whole picture. A scientific 'attitude' can be taken to the study of the whole, as in scientific medical holism.

The combined Hop-Gar Mantis system utilises the scientific method, where appropriate. Beyond this it is 'informed' by science, in the sense that it freely incorporates information and insights gained from bio-mechanics, anatomy, physiology, psychology and anthropology. The scientific attitude is also taken to the testing and development of its basic principles and structure. Therefore, as a style, Hop-Gar Mantis is as scientific as possible, within the limitations of science itself. If demonstrable and scientific reasoning are limited, is there an alternative or complementary rational process available?

Dialectical Reasoning

Where science ends, or can offer no 'proofs', the only rational recourse open is that of pure reason. Traditionally, this is known as 'dialectical reasoning' and is based on the belief that it is possible to discover truth through honest, open and reflective dialogue or debate. Its origins are said to go back to the Greek philosopher Socrates (469-399 BC). Socrates was a soldier as well as a sculptor and a philosopher. His dialectical style, also known as Socratic reasoning, is based on the fundamental principle that the search for truth is a continuous process. Therefore, it doesn't matter at what point you start, even if in error, as the truth may eventually emerge. For this method to work, you have to be prepared to be wrong. It's not about the clever use of words to win an argument by distorting the facts (known as Sophistry to Greek dialecticians), and is certainly not about self-deception through auto-suggestion or agreeable, feeling toned ideas.

Socrates' starting point was always that he 'didn't know', and therefore wished to understand, how it was that others claimed to know things to be true, with certainty. The method draws out inconsistencies in beliefs that would otherwise be hidden, and gradually resolves the picture of a whole situation into a clearer focus. Resistance to using this method is often found in people with fixed emotionally charged ideas. Socrates would travel around Greece challenging the 'wise' to publicly debate with him and prove the certainty of their knowledge; all he knew, he said, was that he didn't know, but gave the immortal advice to Know Thyself! as the ultimate goal of philosophical enquiry. The dialectic is a form of intellectual 'pressure testing', every bit as difficult as the physical kind, perhaps even more so, as who really makes the effort to overcome themselves psychologically? To apply the dialectic to oneself means to constantly challenge your own most heartfelt beliefs. This is the real way to overcome personal limitations.

The Socratic Method in Teaching the Martial Arts

The Socratic method has been applied to education many times in the past but finds its best application in an 'apprenticeship' situation, as can be found in the close personal relationship between teacher and student in the best martial arts schools. Here, the fundamental idea is that the student 'knows the 'truth' but hasn't realised it yet. Therefore, **the teacher works constantly to draw the student's learning and understanding out,** as a kind of personal victory over ignorance.

This is achieved by constantly questioning the student's reasoning, and guiding him to discover (more likely uncover) the truth. In such cases we have a physical as well as an intellectual dialectic, but with the same dynamic at work.

Recently I was interested to read an article by Rorion Gracie (Grappling With Reality part 6) in Inside Kung-Fu magazine: January 1999. Here, he openly advocated the Socratic learning method, and states that it is applied at the Torrance Ju-Jitsu Academy, California.

The dialectic and the resolution of 'opposites' is an interesting aspect of thinking. There is some complementarity between the dialectical method and Eastern ideas on 'opposites'. Later dialectical developments, based on the so-called pre-Socratic Greek philosophers, emphasised the role that opposites have in nature, and the regulation of the universe.

The interaction between opposites was said to be dialectical, in that the polarity created by opposition was resolved into a higher, third position, which transcends the limitations of the original pair, not simply by cancelling each other out, but by the creation of a new factor. This in turn, would meet its opposite and the two would interact dialectically to create yet another position and so on. It's quite easy to see how this relates to Chinese Yin-Yang theory, and western Sinologists (students of Chinese culture) have indeed drawn the parallel.

Formal Logic and the Martial Arts

There is yet another aspect to reasoning that is often employed in structure if not in name within the martial arts; this is so-called formal logic. This derives from the Greek philosopher Aristotle (384-322 BC). Aristotle was the tutor of Alexander the Great, and a grand-student of Socrates. He valued the dialectical method, but wished to formalise logical reasoning, and produced a literal 'formula' in what is known as the syllogism. Essentially it goes like this: all logical arguments or statements can be broken down into three parts. Firstly a major premise, then a minor premise and finally a conclusion. Provided all three elements are present, then the argument is valid. This does not mean that the conclusion is **true**, merely that the structure of the argument is **correct**. If however, the premises are true, then the conclusion necessarily follows i.e. is also 'true'.

In the martial arts, this kind of reasoning is often used to persuade people of the validity of a belief. For example:

Major premise: All traditional martial arts don't work in the street.

Minor premise: Style X is a traditional martial art.

Conclusion: Therefore, style x doesn't work in the street.

Logical isn't it?

This argument is certainly valid, in the sense that it follows the formal rules of syllogistic reasoning. However, it depends on the truth of the major and minor premises for the truth of its conclusion. Can it be really be an objective truth that all traditional martial arts don't work in 'the 'street'?   Part of the art of persuasion is to get a subject to accept some initial premise, and then to link others to it so that any conclusion is automatically accepted, uncritically.   Dialectical reasoning would sort this fallacy out, by uncovering the falseness of the initial premise, and the inadequacy of the conclusion. If properly applied, it would also highlight the real motive behind the framing of such an argument, a result which is likely to be unpopular as people who profess to employ logic seldom enjoy having the role of their personal equation being pointed out.

Beware False Prophets

The martial arts are full of amateur philosophers who profess wisdom, empiricism, science and reasoning. Numbers of such people have no proper philosophical education, and are more like Sophists (see above) than dialecticians. It is better to consider the motives behind a particular line of reasoning than to simply allow oneself to be persuaded through suggestion. If in doubt, try to see the bigger picture. Consider the personal equation (yours and theirs) and apply the dialectic ruthlessly and honestly. Then, if Socrates is right, truth will emerge!

Post-modernity and the philosophy of the martial arts come under the heading of martial arts anthropology. I have written a paper on this subject. Essentially it concerns a contemporary movement in philosophy known as post-modernism, and deals with its relationship to the development and practice of the martial arts. Post-modernism arose during the 1960's and 1970's as a radical philosophy of the arts and social sciences. It rejected the notion of a fixed form or structure, or the certainty of any kind of traditional belief.   In other words, all previous attempts to understand anything, from art to culture, were false, due to inflexibility and the partial truthfulness of the explanations. Eclecticism, the principle of taking what appears to be 'best' from a wide variety of philosophies or systems, is emphasised, as is 'doing your own thing'.

Bruce Lee's Post-Modern Jeet-Kune-Do Eclecticism

In my paper, I attempted for the first time to place Bruce Lee and his conceptual 'non-style' of Jeet-Kune-Do into a contemporary cultural perspective. **His approach is clearly in the post-modern vein, although he himself had no conscious notion of this.** Post-modern martial artists reject classical styles, and fixed systems. They have no time for Kata or form, and encourage an indulgence in eclecticism. My research has shown however that **there is nothing new in this,** indeed it is an ever-present cultural dynamic, that periodically arises to give impetus to generative change, throughout human history. This process is active in all areas of human endeavour, including religion; philosophy and the martial arts, but no-one before has, to my knowledge, specifically identified its role in the evolution and contemporary development of the fighting arts.

For any idea or system to take hold in a culture, it must resolve into something definable and recognisable. In the martial arts, this is found in the creation of any exclusive, single style, or fighting system. This is known as the Monist (from the Greek Monad: single or whole) phase. These fixed styles will eventually create problems for their practitioners, either through generating their own internal inconsistencies, or by collision with other monistic systems that may make similar claims of exclusive martial truth. This is followed by a chaotic phase, characterised as Eclecticism (nowadays called post-modernism) within which a literal feeding frenzy of 'anything that works goes' takes place, with practitioners dissecting the older, monistic systems for useful techniques and ideas.

However, **eclecticism is itself inherently unstable,** and eventually the tension generated must resolve itself into something more regular and systematised, again. This phase is known as the integrative (syncretistic) phase, and may be characterised by what we call today 'combined styles', for example combinations of successful systems that when synthesised, become complementary, adding to one another's strengths and compensating for each others weaknesses. A familiar example would be the combination of Brazilian Ju-Jitsu with Thai-boxing.

The contemporary practice of cross-training can be seen as either eclectic or integrative. Some who call themselves cross-trainers are really pure eclectics, and in effect act culturally to break down our martial arts

---

inheritance.   Other cross-trainers are involved in the cultural process of building up the next phase of development, by championing the synthesis of two or more older monistic systems.   In essence, both are necessary for the continued evolution of the arts, although few individuals are consciously aware of the part that they are playing in this eternal cycle.

Taking an anthropological perspective, it is interesting to note that there is direct evidence for all of these stages in the past history of the arts, although eclecticism has tended to leave little trace of itself.   This is because there is no 'tradition' of eclecticism, only of established monistic styles, and generative new developments, usually arising from a rationalising synthesis of systems that have gone before.   In our contemporary times, we are fortunate to have a very well developed information technology: books, videos, computers and so on, all of which allow us to record the dynamics of evolutionary change in ways undreamed of in the past.

Returning to Jeet-Kune-Do

The theory predicts that **this system will spontaneously generate different versions of itself,** some of which may then be combined with other successful systems, and then to eventually evolve into new, perhaps rival monisms.   **There is already evidence that this is taking place.**   An anthropological awareness allows martial artists to step outside of the fashions and limitations of their own times, and take a fully conscious role in the evolution of their art.

Philosophy and the Combined Hop-Gar Mantis System

Given the undoubted role of eastern philosophy in the development of the oriental martial arts, what specific role does philosophy take in the combined style?   Students are taught the full cultural context for the system, which naturally includes the eastern approach to philosophy. However, the combined style is a western development of traditional Chinese Kung-Fu, and so cannot ignore the western cultural context either.

Students are trained in the Socratic method which they enjoy immensely; and apply it to their physical as well as their mental development. They are taught to reason philosophically, about the style, about themselves, their teachers and the beliefs, opinions and suggestions of others. They are also taught and fully familiarised with the philosophy and anthropology of martial arts evolution, so that they may better understand the culture and the times within which they live. This is the best preparation for 'knowing thyself', which brings us to the next section, mental training.

Mental Training and the Martial Arts

Like philosophy, mental training in the martial arts is a controversial area. Its remit ranges from the simple use of imagery techniques and meditation, through to 'spiritual development' and awareness. Just how much authentic mental training translates into the West from the East is not clear, and its presence should not be taken for granted.

Where spiritual and mental training does exist in the Chinese martial arts, it is usually either in the form of Buddhist or Taoist religion, or the use of respiratory training, chi-gung and 'spirit work' (see traditional training above). Westerners usually develop interest in the formal religious side of Chinese arts independently, motivated by their own desires to study and to learn. They are usually given relatively free access to respiratory training and chi-gung, but seldom if ever to the sun-gung and sun-dar (spiritual work and spirit-attack). I have been involved in the latter, and have been given privileged access to the exercises and to the sacred shrines where individuals call on spirits to inhabit their bodies. At one such location, no other westerner had ever been allowed in before, let alone witness what went on.

An Anthropological Perspective

As a martial arts psycho-anthropologist (the study of the psychology and trans-cultural basis of the martial arts), I take the academic viewpoint that there is nothing different at root between these activities, and other so called 'possession states' found in other cultures in other parts of the world. However, I have the deepest respect for the context of these practices, and note that in their specific form, they belong within the matrix of their originating culture, and not here in the West. It seems then that if you follow a Chinese art, you will need to develop some of your mental and spiritual training away from your specific system or style, although you may usefully study such things as chi-gung and Chinese medicine. **On reflection, I believe it to be right that the "deeper' aspects of Chinese martial-spiritual work are generally denied to westerners,** as the potential for harm or misunderstanding is very real. Thankfully, oriental religions do not require their adherents to be martial artists, and they can be fully experienced without any need to train in the martial disciplines. So what can happen then, when an oriental martial art minus its eastern religious element is assimilated into western culture, and practised by western students?

There is a danger of 'spiritual inflation'. As with all 'flowers' it depends upon the soil in which they are planted. The real key is the psychological state of the individuals concerned. Some won't miss the religious or mental element at all. Others will, as outlined above, follow their own course of study to fill in any gaps. **Some however, run the risk of what is known in depth psychology as spiritual inflation.** This refers to a process whereby a vulnerable personality loses a large measure of its individual identity, and becomes 'puffed-up' with religious ideas. **Martial artists who have been particularly one-sided in their personal development (usually physically-so) are most at risk.** These ideas may be focused in a definite direction, or more usually be diffuse so that ideas about 'God' are hinted at or referred to in an unstructured way. The lack of structure reinforces the 'mystical' almost prophet like quality of their beliefs, which arise in compensation for their previously harsh, and physical approach to their training, and also perhaps to life.

Loss of 'ego' = loss of balance. Sometimes, these people will proudly declare that they have no ego. It is as if they believe that this is a good thing, and worthy of a boast. From a psychological perspective however, such a loss is an unmitigated disaster! The term ego (pronounced 'egg-oh'), is derived from Latin and means 'I'. Its real meaning is the focal point of conscious self-awareness. Nothing can be conscious (made aware), without being associated with the ego. A highly developed self-reflexive consciousness is a human quality achieved only through great personal struggle, both in the life of an individual, and in the evolution of the human species as a whole.   Consciousness is very tenuous, and like a fragile light, it can be easily blown out, by darker and more archaic psychological forces that dwell within us all.

"Nature abhors a vacuum", even a psychological one.   If the 'ego' is deliberately suppressed, then its place will be filled by contents and processes that properly remain unconscious.   The sad thing is that as the 'individual' ego is displaced, the psyche (from the Greek for mind or soul) struggles to contain itself, lest it inflates into a psychotic dissociation. Then, it is usual to find that a transpersonal ego in the form of a 'God' of one kind or another, is utilised to keep the individual personality in a state of balance, or even sanity.

A Tension of Opposites

Usually, where one-sided physical development has become compensated for by a 'discovery' of religion, and/or where an inflated ego has to be checked by a 'God', the personality as a whole settles into a kind of balanced state, wherein the excesses of the individual are controlled to an extent by a religious idea.

However, this polarity is potentially dangerous.   Firstly, such people are very unconscious, and don't 'know themselves' (Socrates).   Secondly, they are likely to become aggressively evangelical about their alleged insights into a 'higher truth'.   Thirdly, they influence others around them through a kind of hypnotic suggestion.   These people may become leaders of cults (of various kinds including martial arts organisations), or eventually 'revert to type' (their true nature), or maybe develop a serious mental illness or personality disorder.

As a consultant psychotherapist in the National Health Service (NHS), I have seen many such people, and indeed I have met their direct equivalents in the world of martial arts. Profound insight of a spiritual or psychological kind is a rarity. There's nothing wrong in this, only in dangerously unbalanced and yet influential people making outlandish claims for themselves, and misleading vulnerable students, some of them children.

The insights potentially afforded by a true immersion into an oriental religion, practised in concert with a martial art, are indeed worthwhile. However, where the necessary discipline is lacking, and apparently replaced by evangelism and prophet like certainty, it may only mask an underlying violent personality disorder, compensated in equal and opposite measures, by the strength of the so-called 'spiritual' or religious, rhetoric.

In the West, there are home-grown traditions of personal development that dovetail very well with the practise of the martial arts as a quest for self-knowledge. These are philosophy, and the discipline of 'depth psychology' or the psychology of the unconscious mind.   Neither is achieved without great effort, an effort that parallels that of the physical in martial training.   The advantage of the western tradition is that it affords no hiding place or refuge for personal limitations.   Followers of these paths are not afforded the luxury of self-deceit through auto-suggestion or emotionally charged ideas.

The Use of Imagery in Mental Training

This has a very long history in all walks of life, and so of course we also find it in the martial arts.   Firstly, we should distinguish between internally generated imagery and the direct mental copying or role modelling that accompanies the learning of any physical skill from a teacher. During the latter, there is a simultaneous mental and physical correspondence involved in the learning process.   However, with internally generated imagery, the body is at rest, with the mind fine-tuned to the 'imaginal rehearsal' and development of skill.

Imaginal rehearsal is a technique developed in clinical psychology for the treatment of phobic anxiety.   However, it is also successfully employed by sports and exercise scientists to improve performance in athletes.   Indeed, I myself have utilised it clinically to assist athletes increase performance at all levels, from beginning martial arts students, through to international competitive body building and Olympic cycling. The difference in my approach is that I employ hypnosis as a vehicle for the imagery techniques, which seems to vastly improve outcomes. In fact, imaginal rehearsal was originally founded by Joseph Wolpe as a hypnotic technique. However, due to political pressures within the disciplines of clinical and experimental psychology, the hypnotic element was dropped in favour of what is now called systematic desensitisation by imaginal rehearsal. But that's another story! Nevertheless, recent research has shown that even rather elementary hypnotic techniques work better than just plain 'imagery' both clinically and in sports science.

One of the most efficient ways to develop martial skill through internally generated imagery is to start with the premise that all perceptions, whether internal or external, must be coded in one or more of the 'senses'. In other words, it is impossible to 'imagine' anything that is not: represented in conscious awareness in one or more of the five physical senses. If you're unsure about this, try it! Anything and everything you can generate as any kind of image must be configured in this way.

The Fallacy of Positive Thinking

In some forms of psychotherapy, patients are told to 'think' differently about a problem, in order to 're-frame' it. This has carried over into sports science, as athletes are encouraged to employ positive thinking, or to develop a positive mental attitude. In a clinical sense, the problem is that positive thoughts have a tendency to spontaneously generate their opposite i.e. negative thoughts. It seems that so-called 'higher' mental processing often works this way, usually to our advantage, as it allows us to consider the pro's and the con's of any given situation. However, in a person who has been overwhelmed by life's demands, it may only serve to generate increased tension, as the natural polarity of consciousness works against itself. This so-called 'cognitive' therapy may work well in some instances, but in others it may make things considerably worse, or at best simply fail. **With individuals who can think clearly, then it is likely to have some good effect.** Here however, much of the success is due to suggestion, that is influence, deriving from either the individual concerned, (auto-suggestion) or from a third party, such as a clinical therapist or a sports coach (hetero-suggestion). This is another good reason to employ hypnotic techniques as they amplify suggestion markedly.

The Primacy of the Senses

But what of people who can't think positively, or who are resistant to cognitive-style suggestion? The emphasis on thinking can be a mistake, as this allows too much room for consciousness to generate resistances. What is needed is a more direct access to experience, that by-passes thinking. In other words, the sensory modalities themselves. In an evolutionary sense (so to speak!) the physical senses developed many millions of years before the human capacity to think consciously.

Therefore, to develop the skill to construct experience coded only in the senses, without any confounding cognitive affects, is very useful. Such imaginal and constructive 'learning' works mainly through the unconscious, and is pre-cognitive. It is well known amongst clinical therapists that this method works incredibly quickly and effectively. Most fears are constructed out of wrongly tuned sensory perceptions. The thoughts follow the senses, they do not lead them. It's the same with athletic performance or the development of fine motor skills such as in the martial arts. Sensory processing has primacy, not thinking.

Martial artists who wish to improve their performance or overcome their fears and anxieties should simply focus on the generation of sensory based imagery that 'codes' for physical success. Space does not here permit a detailed description of the process.

Eastern Meditation

This naturally falls under the remit of mental training, and there are marked differences with the western tradition. Usually there is little emphasis on the improvement of skill, but rather on the development of insight and an attitude of mind. This is the province of religion (see above) and a particularly interesting divergence of opinion arises between the methods and goals of East and West. The western discipline of depth psychology is the psychology of the unconscious mind, and holds that eastern meditative methods do not increase consciousness, but actually lower it! This contradicts received opinion, which sees eastern meditation as a way to increase consciousness.

For the depth psychologist, consciousness is the focus of awareness, with self awareness (the ego) being at its centre. Things can only be conscious to the extent that they are related to the ego. If normal self-reflexive consciousness is lowered, then psychological contents that are normally unconscious come into awareness, and may even occupy it to the extent that consciousness is extinguished. Something like this can happen during eastern style meditation. The trick is to hold the tension between the conscious and unconscious minds so that true insight is gained, rather than the simple assimilation of the ego by the unconscious.

The contents of the unconscious have a peculiar fascination for the conscious ego (rather like being hypnotised). In this suggestible state, the conscious mind may believe that it has superior awareness, but in fact it has merely become just one more item in the store of unconsciousness. The issues are difficult, and require proper guidance.

Hypnosis and the Mind-Body Connection

This is at the cutting edge of development in contemporary medical hypnosis, and concerns the research and clinical application into how hypnosis and natural trance states may be utilised to heal the body of illness. Here again hypnosis has shown its clear superiority as a technique over simple imagery or meditation. As a research area, it should be of interest to martial artists, for the purposes of natural self healing, and also for its insights into chronobiology (body-time) and 'time of day strikes'.

Mental training in the combined Hop-Gar Mantis system is an important factor. My students are exposed to the full remit of mental training systems available, with advanced practitioners being trained in hypnosis up to professional level, giving them membership of externally accredited registers, based on the U.K. government's National Occupational Standards (NOS) for hypnotherapy. Combined with their philosophical education, this makes them very well prepared to meet both psychological as well as physical challenges.

In conclusion, the presence of authentic philosophical or psychological (mental) training, in the martial arts should not be taken for granted. There are many pitfalls and traps awaiting the unwary, and unethical instructors, who are only too happy to exploit people's capacity to employ auto-suggestion to fool themselves.

Martial arts students should be prepared to question their instructors' beliefs and claims to spiritual or psychological knowledge. They should be particularly wary of 'closet psychopaths' who may masquerade as legitimate teachers. This is particularly important where children and young people are concerned.

Students may also usefully research their own cultural background as a matrix for assimilating eastern ideas, thereby maintaining the ancient Greek tradition of tolerance and acceptance, by identifying the deep similarities between cultures, that are often hidden by superficial differences.

Conclusion

This book has introduced the combined Hop-Gar Mantis system of Kung-Fu: a new synthesis of traditional Chinese martial arts with the very best of western science and philosophical reasoning. The Chinese martial arts are a cultural flower, that can only authentically take root in a foreign soil if the ground is prepared and nurtured to receive it. Part of that preparation is the understanding that Kung-Fu will be changed by its assimilation into western culture, and that the direction of that change can be productive, if the benefits already present in the 'soil' are properly utilised.

The new system is born out of 33 years experience of the martial arts, 26 of them in traditional Chinese Kung-Fu, under a total of nine masters. The 'practical' experience upon which the style is based was gained in 13 years of front line Police service, in one of Britain's toughest forces. The inclusion of elements deriving from western science and been based on a lifetime of informal as well as professional education in a wide range of disciplines. This experiential package, drawing together such a wide range of learning, is probably unique in the martial arts, and gives the soundest base for the development and teaching of this most cosmopolitan and yet traditional Kung-Fu style.

Many contemporary issues have been challenged, as have some of the most familiar of traditional beliefs. Students of this system are trained to be efficient thinkers as well as practical fighters. Most importantly they are given the tools to develop as martial artists and as people.

Together, East and West make a whole. They are the opposite sides of the same coin!

Addendum to section page 206:

How are the effects caused ? Well, Western medical anatomists have studied what they call 'trigger points' for many decades. These often correspond directly with acupressure or acupuncture points, and either directly affect the physical area of the point itself, or even have 'referred effects' elsewhere on the body. They are also known to effect thenervous system and organs in the body. Sometimes active trigger points can indicate disease processes in the body, and many Western medical practitioners and physiotherapists are trained to stimulate these points to improve health. There are also the considerable effects of psychology involved.

The main difference between this Western approach and that of the East, is that in the west there is demonstrable scientific and physical evidence for the processes involved, there being no need for superstitious thinking or belief in energy meridians

Steve Richards: Kung Fu Lineage

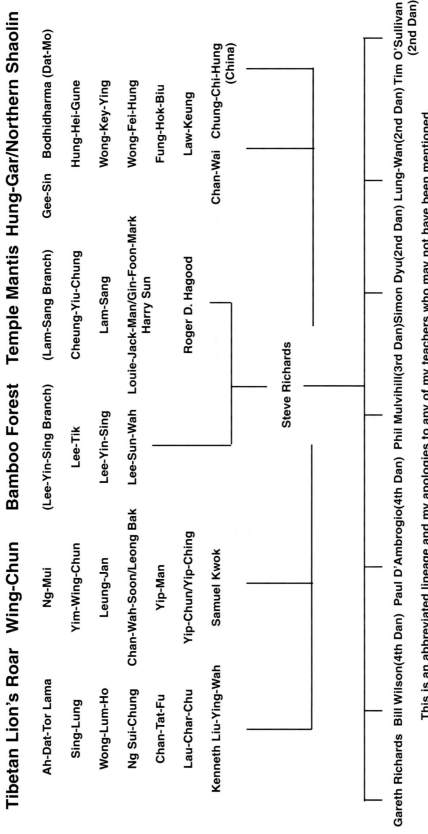

Tibetan Lion's Roar

Ah-Dat-Tor Lama
Sing-Lung
Wong-Lum-Ho
Ng Sui-Chung
Chan-Tat-Fu
Lau-Char-Chu
Kenneth Liu-Ying-Wah

Wing-Chun

Ng-Mui
Yim-Wing-Chun
Leung-Jan
Chan-Wah-Soon/Leong Bak
Yip-Man
Yip-Chun/Yip-Ching
Samuel Kwok

Bamboo Forest

(Lee-Yin-Sing Branch)
Lee-Tik
Lee-Yin-Sing
Lee-Sun-Wah

Temple Mantis

(Lam-Sang Branch)
Cheung-Yiu-Chung
Lam-Sang
Louie-Jack-Man/Gin-Foon-Mark
Harry Sun
Roger D. Hagood

Hung-Gar/Northern Shaolin

Gee-Sin   Bodhidharma (Dat-Mo)
Hung-Hei-Gune
Wong-Key-Ying
Wong-Fei-Hung
Fung-Hok-Biu
Law-Keung
Chan-Wai   Chung-Chi-Hung
                      (China)

Steve Richards

This is an abbreviated lineage and my apologies to any of my teachers who may not have been mentioned.
Claims of legitimate descent must be directly traceable through this lineage for registration purposes:
Amateur Martial Assocation (AMA) British Council for Chinese Martial Arts (BCCMA) Chinese Wu-Shu Research Institute (GB)
British Chin Woo Athletic Association Bamboo Temple Chinese Benevolent Association British Jook-Lum Temple Kung Fu Association
Note: The Lam-Sang branch of Bamboo Forest Temple Mantis is not a part of the Combined Hop-Gar Mantis System.
Lam-Sang-Jook-Lum Mantis is studied and practiced as a separate discipline in its own right.

Gareth Richards Bill Wilson(4th Dan) Paul D'Ambrogio(4th Dan) Phil Mulvihill(3rd Dan)Simon Dyu(2nd Dan) Lung-Wan(2nd Dan) Tim O'Sullivan
(2nd Dan)

Appendix
of
some
of
the
Chinese
names
found
in
this
book

俠家螳螂功夫 ...HOP GAR TONG LONG KUNG FU

連環 ...LIN-WAN - CONTINUOUS AND   RETURNING

驚彈勁 ...GIN-TAN-GING - SUDDEN SHOCK
SPRINGING POWER

俠家 ...HOP GAR

喇嘛派 ...LAMA PAI

白鶴派 ...WHITE CRANE - PAK HOK PAI

入門弟子 ...YUP-MUN-DAI-JI - CLOSED DOOR STUDENT

師傅 ...SI-FU - TEACHER

拜師 ...BAI SI - CEREMONY FOR ACCEPTANCE AS
AN INDOOR STUDENT

靈位 ...SPRI - ALTAR FOR PAYING RESPECTS TO KUNG FU
ANCESTORS

江西竹林螳螂拳 ...KWANGSI JOOK LUM JI LAM
PAI TONG LONG

武館 ...KWOON - TRAINING SCHOOL

鳳眼搥 ...FANG-AN-CHOI - PHOENIX EYE

雞心搥 ---GAI-SUM-CHOI - CHICKEN'S HEART FIST

插搥 ...TSAP CHOI - FORE-KNUCKLE FIST - ALSO GINGER FIST OR GERN CHI CHOI

獅子吼握拳 ...KNUCKLE BASED LION'S ROAR FIST SHAPE

彈腿 ...TAN-TUI - SPRINGING KICK

雙飛腿 ...FAI-TUI - FLYING KICK; ALSO SEUNG: DOUBLE

鏢腿 ...BUI-TUI - DART KICK: ALSO SEUNG: DOUBLE

洪家 ...HUNG GAR (A KUNG FU STYLE)

黃飛鴻 ...WONG FAI HUNG

李賢勝 ...LEE YIN SING

北少林派 ...BAK SIU LUM PAI

詠春派 ...WING CHUN PAI

陳懷 ...CHAN WAI - JIMMY CHAN

鄭忠 ...JOSEPH CHENG

何勝　　　...HO SING

李新華　　...LEE SUN WAH

廖應華　　...KENNETH LIU YING WAH

廖應山　　...NICHOLAS LIU YING SAN

精武体育會　...CHING WOO ATHLETIC ASSOCIATION

廖應仁　　...PHILIP LIU

獅子吼　　...LION ROAR

氣　　　　...CHI - INTERNAL ENERGY

針灸　　　...ACUPUNCTURE

講手　　　...GONG SAU - HARD HAND REAL FIGHTING

師弟 ...SI-DAI

師兄 ...SI-HING

大師兄 ...DAI-SI-HING

南獅 ...SOUTHERN LION

麒麟 ...UNICORN

郭思牧 ...SAMUEL KWOK

西藏 ...TIBET

撞 ...CHON - TO DESTROY

穿 ...CHUNE - TO PENETRATE

截 ...JEET - TO INTERCEPT

閃 ...SIM - TO EVADE OR AVOID AN ATTACK

HOP GAR MANTIS KUNG FU • A SCIENCE OF COMBAT

Notes

Notes

Notes

Notes